Social Casework

Social Casework

A Therapeutic Approach

R.K. Upadhyay

RAWAT PUBLICATIONS
Jaipur • New Delhi • Bangalore • Guwahati • Kolkata

ISBN 978-81-7033-758-4 (HB)

Reprinted, 2022

Published by
Prem Rawat for **Rawat Publications**
Satyam Apts., Sector 3, Jawahar Nagar, Jaipur - 302 004 (India)
Phones: 0141 265 1748 / 265 7006
E-mail : info@rawatbooks.com
Website: rawatbooks.com

New Delhi Office
4858/24, Ansari Road, Daryaganj, New Delhi 110 002
Phone: 011-23263290

Also at *Bangalore, Guwahati and Kolkata*

Typeset by Rawat Computers, Jaipur
Printed at Nice Printing Press, New Delhi

Contents

Acknowledgement

I am grateful to my students and colleagues who inspired me to write this book. In my efforts to write this book, I am thankful to Prof. C.P. Goyal for discussing the case record (produced in the book) with me. I am deeply indebted to Shri K.B. Gulati who took pains to type and re-type the manuscript whenever required.

I am thankful to my family members, especially my wife, for keeping me free from the domestic work which helped me to execute this work satisfactorily.

In the end, I wish to thank the publisher who has undertaken the task thereby serving the cause of students, practitioners and educators.

R.K. Upadhyay

Preface

In the last decade, sincere attempts were made to promote the professional aspects of social work practice and education in India. Various seminars, conferences and workshops have invariably sought to emphasise the professional contents of social work practice. Fieldwork has been assigned pivotal role in the training of social work. Against this background, literature on social work has covered only the knowledge part of it. The process part of it has remained more or less neglected. To me, social work consists more in the process (how) than in the knowledge derived from various disciplines. The knowledge scanned from various disciplines is only to strengthen and augment the practice of social work method(s), the core of professionalism. Whatever be the field/area of operation, social workers help people to learn new behaviours beneficial in copying with their environment and/or to change or modify the environment itself to meet the needs of the individual to live a personally happy and socially useful life.

It is only with this in view that the present work has been undertaken, for which the students of social work too have been persistently looking for. The students have a few books only on methods by Indian authors to depend upon. Most of the books are by western authors, with exorbitant price beyond the reach of an average Indian student, and practitioners to equip them with necessary knowledge of practice.

How far this attempt has been successful will be known only after the feedback is received from the readers, the students in particular. Attempts have been made to include all relevant topics taught usually under the nomenclature, "working with people-individuals" in social work course. Latest books have been consulted and quoted to acquaint the readers with the recent trends in field. An attempt has also been made to trace the history of social work and casework practice in India alongwith various Vedantic concepts in casework practice. Use of these concepts (and more to be gleaned from other Indian scriptures) will Indianise casework meaningfully. The selection of concepts included in 'Knowledge for Practice' is based on my experience of teaching and practising of social casework. Towards the end of the book, a chapter on unitary approach has been added for the benefit of the readers who may see if unitary approach needs separate teaching and practice. Similarly, a chapter on social work has been given in the beginning of the book to enable the readers to understand the social work perspective.

The author wishes to express his heartfelt thanks to Shri K.B. Gulati, whose untiring efforts (in typing the manuscript) have made the publication of this book possible. My thanks are also due to Dr. Sandhya, my daughter and Lecturer (Social Work) who helped me at various stages of preparing the manuscript.

1

Social Work: A Helping Process

Social work, a service to maintain society's harmonious functioning, is basically a helping process. It finds a specific mention in the Vedic (*Rigveda*) word, 'dānam', which reflects the social philosophy of those days to help the needy members of the society. The helping process through *dān* seems to have found due recognition during that period when *Rigveda* (VIII 6.5 & X 117.6) declares that "the riches of one who gives do not diminish... The solitary eater is also a solitary sinner". In the *Bhagwad Gita*, dānam, i.e., charity is described in terms of material aid, knowledge (*vidya*) and protection against fear, i.e., 'abhaydān. The helping process got further support in Gita's principle of *aparigrah* and the concept of *loksangrah* which mean that materials and money should not be collected for self, and that one should work for the welfare of the community, respectively. Lord Buddha also talked of welfare of the masses (बहुजन हिताय, बहुजन सुखाय). The concept of helping contained in the concept of *dān* got further boost in the Kautilya's *Arthashastra* which holds the king responsible for care and protection of the helpless, the weak, the aged, and also the members of the families of the decreased soldiers and workers. During Ashoka's times, helping process got institutionalised in the appointment of 'Gopas' (social workers) who kept records of castes, births, marriages and looked after people when sick.

Officers-in-charge of liquor and prostitutes were responsible for helping the victims of these social evils too. One of the edicts on pillars by King Ashoka that "...I consider the promotion of the people's welfare my highest duty...", gives a clear picture of welfare activities during his time. Islam also prescribes 'zaka' (charity). Similarly, in British India and in England and USA, people helped the needy individuals and the destitutes out of humanitarian, religious and philanthropic motives.

It was the Association for Improving Conditions of the Poor (AICP) in USA, founded in 1843, which recognised that mere charity does not and cannot solve the problems of the unprivileged and the unfortunates as this approach of helping through charity created a permanent liability on society. The beneficiaries of charity, because of being dependent on it, lose their self-respect and endure on charity for their whole of life. This was against the democratic values. AICP emphasised self-respect, self-dependence and relief suitable to their needs in its work with the poor. This can be said to be the beginning of professionalisation of charity work, done in the name of social work, under Elizabethan Poor Law of 1601, in the colonial USA. The Charity Organisation Society (1877, USA), a voluntary organisation, adopted a scientific approach to determine the applicant's needs after investigation through the help of 'friendly visitors'. Thus, the emphasis in helping process shifted from relief to understanding of the causes of the situation, and the applicants were regarded as victims of their conditions.

The beginning of a more formal and systematic approach to deal with society's problems came with the establishment of National Conference of Charities and Corrections (NCCC), a forerunner of National Conference on Social Welfare. In 1893, the need for educating social workers (i.e., helpers) by their predecessors was endorsed by Anna L. Dawas. In 1897, Mary Richmond pleaded to teach common elements of 'charity work' at a school by field supervisors. Towards the end of 19th century, the New York School of Philanthropy began to train the investigatory personnel of the charity organisations.

In social work education, it was casework, which emerged first and remained the sole method of social work till the beginning of 1940s when group work and community organisation were added to its dictionary. Casework, which was mentioned as "work with cases" in the proceedings of the National Conference in the late 1890s, "became a well-defined technique in 1911". In 1917, Mary Richmond published the first book on social casework under the title, *Social Diagnosis.* Education for social work became a two-year programme around 1910 and schools of social work were opened at Boston and Chicago, etc. We thus find that the work for the society's welfare (helping the needy) started in the form of charity which achieved the status of a profession only in the beginning of the present century.

The nature of social work, now a full-fledged profession, has been explained by Boehm (1958) in the following words: "Social work seeks to enhance the social functioning of individuals, singly and in groups, by activities focused upon their social relationships which constitute the interaction between man and his environment. These activities can be grouped into three functions: restoration of impaired capacity, provision of individual and social resources, and prevention of social dysfunction." Social work, as a profession, is no more interested in charity and relief work: instead, it is concerned with the social functioning of the individuals.

Social functioning, i.e., functioning in social roles, comprises all those activities that are essential to "satisfying relationship in the variety of experience of social living". Every member of the society continues to function in some role or other and any obstacle to role performance by the individual creates a problem in social functioning. Social work considers an individual's relationship with other human being as its primary unit of attention. How and with what effectiveness an individual performs his various social roles is the main focus of social work intervention. (Role is a set of socially expected behaviour of a person occupying a particular status in society like a teacher, student, client, etc.). The social worker analyses the individual's social relationship pattern and works through the factors that block the social functioning. According to Bartlett (1970), social functioning consists of interaction between "the coping activity of people and the demand from the environment". The need for enhancement of social functioning should be perceived either by the individual or by the people concerned with him.

The basic functions of a helping process are:

1. restoration,
2. provisions of resources, and
3. prevention.

Restoration has been sub-divided by Skidmore and Thackery (1982) into *curative* and *rehabilitative* forms of activities. In curative, efforts are made to eliminate those factors which cause or precipitate the breakdown of social functioning. Under the rehabilitative activities included are reorganising and rebuilding the interactional patterns of the individual.

Provision of resources too, according to them, has two aspects: *developmental* and *educational*. Enhancing the effectiveness of existing social resources (counselling, medical, Red Cross facilities or personal capacity) to help the individual to function meaningfully in his role is developmental. Informing the public about specific conditions and needs for developing or enriching new social resources through lectures, films, seminars, posters, etc., is included in the educational resources.

The third function, i.e., prevention of social dysfunction, comprises of early detection, elimination of conditions, situations that have potentialities to affect social functioning adversely. Prevention can be either in the realm of problems occurring in the interaction between different systems, or social ills like beggary, dowry, alcoholism, etc.

According to Pincus and Minahan (1973), social work is "concerned with the interaction between people and their social environment which affects the ability of people to accomplish their life tasks and realise their aspirations and values".

Social work, thus, seeks to:

1. enhance the problem-solving and coping capacities of people;
2. link people with systems (organisation) that provide them with resources, services and opportunities;
3. promote the effective and humane operation of these systems; and
4. contribute to the development and improvement of social policy.

Accordingly, the functions of social work have been outlined by Pincus and Minahan (1973) as follows:

1. help people enhance and more effectively utilise their own problem-solving and coping capacities;
2. establish initial linkage between people and resource systems;
3. facilitate interaction and modify and build new relationships between people and society and its resource systems;
4. contribute to the development and modification of social policy;
5. dispense material resources; and
6. serve as agents of social control.

These functions are carried out by someone or other in the society but none performs all these functions in a cluster. Similar view has been expressed by Bartlett (1970) also when she says that social work is "a configuration of elements none of which is unique but which in combination, represent a contribution quite distinct from that rendered by any other profession".

Social worker's focus is upon helping people to improve their social functioning, i.e., their ability to interact and relate to others. While helping individuals to solve their personal problems, and meet their needs, the social worker works with them on conscious level. Since social work recognises the multiplicity of causation of problems, it is concerned with both giving personal help to clients in need of service and with measures that aim at changing the societal conditions (macro-level) causing or contributing to human suffering and maladjustment. In working towards the social adjustment of the individual and of the group, social work needs to consider the socio-cultural environment from which the individual clients and group members come. The objective of social work remains to help individuals and groups to find the best way for their satisfying accomplishment without curtailing their freedom of choice of action unless this violates the well-being and rights of others. It is an art of helping people to help themselves, an art of enabling people to perform their roles properly and live a personally gratifying life in consonance with social requirements.

Social work as a profession, to start with, emphasised the 'social' aspects of the problem. The individual was diagnosed in terms of his relationship with others and his social situation. Richmond (1922) described diagnosis as an "attempt to make as exact a definition as possible of the situation and the personality of a human being in some social needs". Family was very much emphasised. Around 1920, the Freudian psychological theories started affecting social work practice and there was "a radical shift from the consideration of environmental factors to the preoccupation with the intrapsychic. Freudian theory over-shadowed all other approaches to social problems and orientations about behaviour" (Goldstein, 1973). The effect of Freudian theories on social work practice slowly started decreasing with the advent of neo-Freudians like Adler, Fromm Sullivan etc. Social work under the influence of these authors once again, resumed its 'social' focus in its work. In the 1960s 'social' of social work got further boost because of emphasis on *developmental* aspects (as opposed to *residual*) of social welfare.

The *residual* notion of social welfare, based on humanitarian and altruistic attitudes, holds that an individual's needs should be met through social welfare services when they are not met through other societal institutions like family and market economy. Welfare services, according to this view, should be provided only when all other measures have proved to be ineffective, and individual's and his family resources have been exhausted. These are to be given on a short-term basis only. This view holds that welfare programmes are to meet the emergency needs of the normally working individuals. It is to ameliorate the problems of the 'unfortunates'. It is regarded as a source of supplementary rehabilitative service to be utilised when regular social processes breakdown. This approach is based on the assumption that adequately functioning individuals and social institutions do not need social welfare services...that the human problems...are product of accidental or temporary circumstances with which the clients are unprepared to cope with (Grosser, 1976). Residualists believe that our social system has productive and constructive purposes, inequities in our system are unintentional, reasons for the individual's difficulty are contained in his personality, and individual's predicament is the result of his own fault and his personal inadequacy or wrong decisions.

Social work, under residual approach, undertook restorative and rehabilitative functions through social casework, social group work, and community organisation with emphasis on coordination, fund raising, planning, education and guidance etc. The role of social worker as community organiser was considered to be basically that of an enabler who facilitates leadership and develops consensus on the matter of direction, and guides the interaction of the members. Social workers considered client as someone not equal to them and pleaded for an objective and non-partisan approach.

Developmental or *institutional* concept of social welfare is based on the presumption that every citizen requires (or may require) different types of social services "to develop his capacity to perform productive roles and to achieve and maintain a desirable standard of well-being" (Romanyshyn, 1971). Problems are seen as rooted in the social system and in the individual. Inequities are usually subscribed to the intentional and deliberate acts by individuals, various groups and institutions. The beneficiaries are not considered as damaged either psychologically or socially. The individual is helped to "contend with rather than accept his environment". Emphasis is placed on planning, social change, use of resources to maintain and enhance individual's functioning in various social roles alongwith counselling and therapy. This view seeks fullest development of individual by reconstructing his social environment. Efforts are made to develop the human being of the kind we desire and the social structure we need to achieve the desired goal (to maximise development of human potentials). Under this view, the recipient is not stigmatised because it is his right to ask for such services which should be given to them on the pattern of social services. Social worker, consequently, works in the role of advocate, social broker, social planner and activist alongwith in the role of an enabler. The so-called objectivity is substituted in some roles by partisan activities. This perspective helps the social worker to emphasise institutional and policy changes, proper use of resources and their development and to humanise the society for improving the quality of human beings. Social welfare services, in developmental sense, are directed to self-fulfilment. Social work, under this approach, tries to change agencies and institutions, their policy and service delivery patterns to suitably meet the needs of the target group.

However, we see that developmental view does not preclude the residual view. Developmental view simply supplements the residual view by persuading the agencies and institutions to make concessions and deliver services as a permanent and enforcable right of the benefactors.

Social work is practised primarily through its three methods, viz., social casework, social group work, and community organisation, though unitary (integrated) approach has also been adopted by some. Unitary approach does not recognise "three method conception of practice"; rather it looks at social work as one method, i.e., social work method. Since the book is on social casework, a brief description of other two methods is given below.

Community organisation is one of the main methods of social work. It is an inter-group process that seeks to help communities to understand and assess their existing problems and needs and to appropriate the available resources "to bring about solutions that will strengthen the total community and enrich the life of its members". According to Zastrow (1978), "it is a process of stimulating and assisting the local community evaluate, plan and coordinate its efforts to provide for the community's health, welfare and recreation needs".

Community organisation, according to Ross (1967) is "a process by which a community identifies its needs or objectives, orders (or ranks) these needs or objectives, develops the confidence and will to work at (them), finds the resources (internal and/or external) to deal with (them), takes action with respect to them, and in so doing extends and develops cooperative and collaborative attitudes and practices in the community". Community organisation process equips the community "to identify and deal co-operatively and skillfully with its common problems". Community organisation is practised for providing (1) the community or its sections with opportunities to mobilise its resources to tackle social problems or prevent their onset; (2) means for meaningful interaction between different sections of the community; and (3) welfare planning service to the community through development of social welfare plans, influencing welfare policies and mobilising adequate finances from voluntary and public sectors.

Community organisation adopts three modes to fulfil its objectives: (1) locality development which seeks effective community change through wide public participation in every phase of planning and action, as we commonly see in different areas of community development; (2) social planning, understood as a process, which seeks to solve problems like delinquency, mental diseases, etc.; and (3) social action which seeks to organise the disadvantaged or underprivileged group to get due representation in policy-making bodies of the community and proper distribution of community resources. In all these processes, the worker functions as enabler, therapist, educator, advocate, social planner, activists and social broker.

The commonly utilised activities (processes or steps) in community organisation process are study, analysis, assessment, organisation, action and evaluation, or, according to some, these (stages) are exploration, assessment and planning, action and evaluation.

Another method of social work, i.e., *social group work*, seeks to enhance the social functioning of individuals through experience of interacting in group situations. Group experience is administered in a definite way to help the members to achieve their socially sanctioned and personally desired objectives, and to actualise their potentialities for self-development. Group experience consists of interactions with members and others concerned with its members' functioning. The interactions are generated through activities of different kinds, e.g., games, educational discussions, cultural activities, etc. The interaction of members is guided according to the values and principles of social work. Principles for group work practice (specific) are different than the generic principles applied to the practice of all the methods. Group work has basically two purposes: to develop the individuals (developmental approach) in agencies like community centres, social institutions, project centres, etc., and to treat them (clinical approach) like delinquents, emotionally disturbed persons, addicts, etc., through quick group experience.

Group worker either works with the already existing group or with the one that he forms for this purpose. Every group decides its goal in consonance with the agency aims. The usual factors considered in group formation are age, common problems, intellectual level, sex and value system etc. A group larger than 8 to 10 members is difficult to manage and guide. The group worker needs skills in (a) involving members, (b) decision-making about goals, norms and role assignment to its members, (c) group discussion, and (d) planning for meetings. The group worker assumes the role of consultant, facilitator, and coordinator. Knowledge of individual and group behaviour is very important to work with groups. Enabling, as compared to authoritative or manipulative, is a preferred approach. Group work can be practised in all settings, be it correctional, psychiatric, medical, welfare or community setting. Specific techniques are focusing, individualizing, sub-grouping, re-directing, conflict-resolving, programming, norm-setting, equalising etc. With the help of these techniques, guided group interaction enriches the individual's capacity to relate with others, fulfil his needs and learns to live a "personally satisfying and socially useful life".

Now, the following chapters will present knowledge for practice, discuss relationship, communication, interviewing and recording in social case work practice, and, examine the process of helping individuals (social casework) primarily in the residual context, and only towards the end, an overview of unitary and other models in social work will be presented for a fuller view of the social work practice.

2

Social Casework: Nature, Values, Principles and Trends

Social casework was practised in India under the cover of religious and social sermons. Indians had their own ways to achieve and accomplish the individual purposes. It is not surprising and unnatural to find traces of social casework in any culture as every culture has its own ways to deal with and tackle the individual's sufferings and problems. This is very much true of Indian culture too which becomes clear from our various scriptures where the most common techniques used to help the individual clients have been (1) story-telling, (2) imparting knowledge, (3) prayer, (4) yogic exercises, (5) fasting, (6) learning and practising behaviour in the company of saintly persons, and (7) demonstration or modelling behaviour (setting examples), though in *Gita*, Lord Krishna has used techniques of re-educating, informing, imparting knowledge, clarifying the reality to enable Arjuna to perform his roles.

These techniques of helping individuals could not be popular perhaps because these were available only in Sanskrit---a language of elite in those days of India. It remained confined only to certain class of people and certain areas of nation. And, even during the British rule, only few attempted to present it into a systematic way for the consumption of common people. We were encouraged under the then policies of education to study English and import knowledge available in English from the western hemisphere. This happened in those subjects also where we had enough to go by, perhaps because, we wanted to be like our rulers to get rid of our inferiority feelings, to please them and also acquire materials of comforts and fame in the British circles. It is because of these and many other such reasons that we (the educated) copied British ways of life, their language and various aspects of their culture. This tendency probably was further accentuated by the work of missionaries whose converts became 'Madam' and 'Sir' in no time. All these and many other factors kept us away from our own cultural treasures. In the chapters to follow, a very modest attempt has been made to discuss some of the valuable Upnishadic ideas and concepts helpful for social casework practice.

Social casework of today is not totally different from our traditional (scripture-described) approach to individual problem. Our own system of casework like the present one has been very rational and based on intellectual and logical discussions leading to knowledge of reality, self-control and practice of a constructive and socially useful model of behaviour. The accent in our scriptural approach was more on the social aspect of the personality, i.e., the person should conform to the social standards and derive pleasure by contributing significantly to the growth of and harmony in the society. Casework as practised today by the professional social workers also emphasises the social aspects of the case.

Social casework, as taught today in Indian schools of social work, has been imported from the West, specially from USA. We continue to change our syllabi of social work as per the changes occurring in USA and western world. Of late, social work has undergone some changes in the West. Consequently, in place of social casework, social group work and community organisation, an integrated approach (to be discussed separately) has been adopted by many of the schools of social work there. However, in India, the old model of social work teaching and practice is continuing and social casework, social group work and community organisation are being taught as methods of working with people---individual, group and community---as before.

History of Social Casework

The poor, from the very beginning of the civilised society, have been the concern of humanists, philanthropists and socio-religious activists. Its description is found in the Vedic literature (as mentioned in Chapter 1) and of course much later in the western countries. Casework as practised today, a purely western (predominantly USA) model, too owes its history to work by individuals and organisations with the poor. The Association for Improving the Conditions of the Poor (AICP) founded in 1843 in USA, emphasised self-respect, self-dependence and relief suitable to their needs in its work with the poor. The approach behind this service by AICP had a clear departure from the earlier services to the poor in colonial America under Elizabethan Poor Law of 1601, etc., which was based on the concept of charity. Seeds of social casework seems to have been shown with the individualised services of Thomas Chalmers (1780-1847) followed by the Charity Organisation Society (COS) of 1869 (London) and 1877 (USA) respectively. Their work involved investigation to determine clients' needs, central registration, recording, relief giving and use of volunteer, i.e., friendly visitor. Friendly visitors of COS (USA) discovered that all the poor were---not alike and that they should be treated differently. Papers presented at the National Conference of Charities and Corrections enunciated and emphasised the principle of individualisation. COS was asked to reach the individual and restore his function without bothering for detection of imposters on relief. Thus, the concept of scientific charity came into practice and it was recognised that "the poor, and those in trouble worse than poverty, have not, in common, any type of physical, intellectual or moral development which would warrant an attempt to group them as a class".

Friendly visitors at a later stage received training in investigation, diagnosis and treatment for which the New York School of Philanthropy was established towards the end of 19th century (Bruno, 1957) and it was during this time that term 'casework' appeared in a paper read at a national conference. The COS movement gave birth to Family Welfare Association in 1905. In England, around the end of the 19th century, outside visitor (called almoner) at the instance of Sir Charles Loch came to help hospitals to serve their patients effectively. The almoner, like paid agents and friendly visitor of USA, can be said to be the predecessor of caseworker. The almoner's original assignment was seen as the prevention of abuse of hospital treatment. By 1911, social casework had emerged in USA as an accepted formal technique though the first book on social casework was published in 1917 by an American, Marry Richmond. Various definitions of casework in the 1920s under the influence of Freudian theory no more emphasised external factors. It held the individual responsible for his plight and it was he who was helped to cope with the social problems confronting him. During the same time, social reforms and social problems received little attention compared to its earlier period when the emphasis was on correcting the social environment of the client. In 1920s, under the Freudian influence, casework was to "untangle and reconstruct the twisted personality" and change human attitudes so that the client could adjust to his environment and its influence.

In contrast to the trend in 1920s, caseworkers shifted their focus in 1930s from individual to modification and manipulation of the client's environment to enable him to adapt to his situations satisfactorily. This change was because of acceptance of the idea by Americans that social and economic variables influenced man's behaviour meaningfully.

After World War II, with the problems of morale, leadership, propaganda, separation, communication, etc., social workers found social sciences more useful. Interest in social environment, alongwith ego psychology, received more attention and the definition of Richmond (1922) that casework consists of "those processes which develop personality through adjustments consciously effected, individual by individual, between man and their social environment" was considered to be the best by Hamilton (1951). Perlman (1957) also emphasised on the problems of social functioning.

Though many may not agree, I personally think that the latest thinking in casework is more or less fully contained in the definition by Boehm (1958) which emphasises both external and internal factors, and uses the concepts of social functioning, social role, malfunctioning, and, of resources. Many new trends are coming forth and possibly no definition will ever be able to cover all the changes and trends emerging from time to time.

Nature

Social casework, as taught and practised in India today, is understood as an approach to help individuals but not at random. As a method of social work profession, it seeks to help individuals in a systematic way based on knowledge of human behaviour and various tested approaches.

Every individual, child or adult, in order to grow and develop, has various needs (psychological, physical and social) to fulfil. In this task, he has to interact with different types of people and face different environmental conditions. Very often, the individual fails in his attempts fully or partially and sometimes, he has to face non-helpful reactions of the people around him. Lack of resources, non-fulfilment of needs, unpleasant social reactions and unfavourable physical conditions make human development and functioning (i.e., adaptation) difficult and sometimes impossible. An individual, under these stressful conditions, seeks help, sometimes from the near and dear ones (like parents, siblings, friends, etc.) and sometimes from the professionals (priests, teachers, lawyers, doctors, social workers, etc.) Every professional's help has two components: one, his professional skills and knowledge, and the other is his personal characteristics and experiences of life. These two components set the way the professional helper will move to help the needy individual to meet his needs or solve his problems to live a full life. What aspects of life will be aided by whom will depend upon the professional expertise of the person in the helping role. For example, a physician will help only with physical problems, a teacher with educational problems and a lawyer with the legal problems. Social workers help the total individual, i.e., with every aspect of life which, in any way, is detrimental to his living a full life—a life wherein one is not uncomfortable with the happenings in and around him.

Perlman (1957) tries to understand this process of helping individuals in terms of a person with a problem, who comes to a place (an agency) where a professional representative (trained person) helps him by a given process. She thus delineates the four basic components of social casework, viz., person, problem, place (agency) and process. She explains that problems arise from some needs or obstacles to the fulfilment of these needs, or accumulation of frustrations, or maladjustment, or sometimes from all of these put together. These individually or together threaten or have already attacked the person's living arrangement or the effectiveness of his efforts to deal with it. These problems are tackled through a process which is a progressive transaction between the professional (trained) helper and clients. It consists of problem-solving operations carried on within a meaningful relationship (purposefully established). These operations aim at developing the client's effectiveness in coping with his problem and/or so influence the problem as to resolve or vitiate its effect. The person is the one who is "in need of help in some aspect of his social-emotional living, whether the need be for tangible provisions or counsel". As he begins to receive such help, he is called, 'client'. The place is "a social service agency or a social service department of another kind or a human welfare agency". Perlman (1957) thus defines social casework as a "process used by certain human welfare agencies to help individuals to cope more effectively with their problems in social functioning".

The concept of 'social functioning' has gained quite an important place in social casework. This concept fully explains the meaning of the adjective, 'social', used with the word 'casework' and helps in differentiating it from psychowork, i.e., psychotherapy.

Social casework enables an individual to obtain a higher level of social functioning through an interpersonal transaction or face-to-face, or person-to-person encounter. The caseworker helps the client to act in order to achieve some personal/social goals by utilising the available resources in terms of strength of personality of the client, his social system or material provisions available in the community and/or agency. Caseworker's knowledge and expertise, and material resources are used (as tools) to inject strengths in the person to enable him to move more satisfyingly in the social situation he finds difficult to deal with.

Richmond (1917), who gave a scientific status to casework, defines social casework as one consisting of "those processes which develop personality through adjustments consciously effected, individual by individual, between man and their social environment". Regensurg (1938) considers casework as a method of "measuring against reality the client's capacity to deal with his problem or pieces of it, while the worker helps him to clarify what the problem is and enables him to think of different ways to solve it". According to Bowers (1949), "social casework is an art in which knowledge of the science of human relations and skills in relationship are used to mobilise capacities in the individual and resources in the community appropriate for better adjustment between the client and all or any part of his total environment". Hamilton (1951) says that casework is "characterised by the objective to administer practical services and offer counselling in such a way as to arouse and conserve the psychological energies of the client—actively involve him in the use of the service toward the solution of his dilemma". These definitions have attempted to focus on certain aspects of casework process only, and when these are taken and understood together, explain the nature of casework better.

Boehm (1959) explains the nature of social casework with due emphasis on social and psychological aspects of human functioning. According to him, social casework intervenes in the psycho-social aspects of a person's life to improve, restore, maintain or enhance his social functioning by improving his role performance. Intervention occurs when the person or members of his group or community realise that his (person) role performance is hampered or threatened. The intervention takes place through a professional relationship between the worker and the person and also between the worker and other individuals whose interaction with the person affects his role performance. Since social functioning is product of interaction among intrapsychic, somatic and social forces, social casework involves assessing the internal and social factors which impair or threaten the person's role performance and helps him to find and use the somatic, psychic and social resources at his disposal to eliminate or reduce malfunction and to enhance functioning in social roles.

A person is the net product of interaction between biological, psychological and environmental (social and physical) factors. The unique pattern that emerges from this interaction is his personality which comprises of his capacities and abilities, attitudes, beliefs and values, feelings, and thinking and his approach, or strategies to deal with various situations of life. Individual problems may arise either because of his unsuitable approach to social situations he encounters in his life or because of situations demanding something different or more than he possesses. Both the situations have social and psychological components, therefore, these form psycho-social aspects of his life. Anything that is social, will evoke psychological responses, similarly anything (thinking and feeling) that is occurring at the level of psyche (i.e., psychological), is bound to show in one's social life (verbal or non-verbal interaction). Psyche always works in social context, therefore, his behaviour (social functioning) has both psychological as well as social components. The caseworker intervenes (helps) in any or all of these aspects to enable the person to function adequately and properly in his various social roles.

A person, at every point of the day, performs some role. All his functions are directed to fulfil some role. The caseworker may mainly aim at restoring, maintaining or improving the person's functioning (performance in different roles ascribed to or achieved by him) using his knowledge of human behaviour, skills in communication and relationships and the available resources. It is presumed that any person who has some problem with his thinking (cognitive), feeling (affect) or acting or their interaction will not be able to function properly and adequately in his social roles (like that of a father, chairman, citizen, man, scientist, etc.) assigned to or achieved by him.

Social functioning means functioning in different roles one has achieved or has been assigned by society according to his position. Bartlett (1970) defines social functioning as "the interaction between the coping activity of people and the demand from the environment". The caseworker does not offer help to the person only at his personal request but also when the person does not seek/or resists help. In such cases help is offered at the instance of his relatives, public agencies (police, hospitals, etc.) or community members who feel concerned and are interested to help the person to live a socially useful life. Caseworker, in addition to the person in need of help, may work with those people also who are in some way or other important for solution of the person's problems. The help is offered through a particular process as mentioned before. This process is usually termed as study, diagnosis (assessment), formulation of goals and planning, treatment, evaluation and termination. Taber & Taber (1985) use Sipron's formulations which are termed as (1) engagement, (2) exploration, (3) planning, (4) intervention, (5) evaluation, and (6) disengagement. Engagement is equivalent to intake, exploration to study, planning involves assessment and planning for action, intervention is equivalent to treatment and evaluation is done after intervention, followed by termination (disengagement) when the purpose of the client has been served. One can reformulate these phases as engagement, exploration (study), assessment (diagnosis), planning (inclusive of goal-setting), intervention, evaluation and follow up, and disengagement.

Thus, social casework, as a helping process, tries to effect a change in the client's behaviour systematically to enable him to achieve what he really needs and to realise his potentials for "living a personally satisfying and socially useful life". And, in this process of helping the client, he offers concrete (protective) services including money and materials, modifies his environment to provide an environment favourable to the required change in him, strengthens and augments his capacities, develops an attitude congenial for growth, effects the desired change in his lifestyle and maintains his emotional equilibrium.

Values

Social casework (or social work) values have roots in the democratic social system. These contain certain ideas which are valuable to anyone engaged in social work practice. It is precisely lack of these values which prohibits practice of social work in socialist societies like China, etc. The values are:

1. *Every man has inherent worth and dignity.* This is a fundamental value of democracy, therefore, of social work too. He or she is worth caring for the simple reason that he/she is an individual, a human being capable of contributing to the growth of society. It is because of this value that social workers attend to every person's need without any consideration of class, caste or creed etc., and serve anyone and everyone without any discrimination. They recognise the fact that every member, whatever be his handicap, has worth; therefore, he deserves to be respected and he is a dignified member of the society like anyone of the society. He had to be respected so that he can get all possible help and facilities to live a socially productive and personally gratifying life.
2. From this it follows that *individual has right to self-determination*, taking decisions about all the matters related to self as long as it does not interfere with the rights of others. One is considered to be capable of taking decisions about one's own future and the helper is only to tell him the pros and cons of his decisions to enable him to choose his own future course of action.
3. *Every individual is the primary concern of society, has potential for and the right to growth* and it is the responsibility of the society to provide equal opportunities to everyone to actualise his self.
4. *Every individual, in turn, has to contribute to the society's development* by assuming his social responsibility, discharging his functions honestly and acting properly and adequately in his social roles.
5. *The individual and society in which one lives are interdependent.* Neither the individual nor the society can be conceived of without each other.

6. *Basic human needs have to be met by services* which are not contingent upon conformity either to moral behaviour or to race, nationality, religion, caste, etc.

Assumptions

These are theoretical concepts (an idea or set of ideas or thoughts) which are accepted as true about the human beings functioning. These give us a frame of reference to understand man in interaction with his environment and help in exploration (study) and diagnostic evaluation of the cases. These are:

(1) *Man is a bio-psycho-social being who is in constant interaction with his environment.* Social functioning is determined by this interaction. When the child is born, he is nothing but a mere organism capable of bare minimum physiological processes. Mother starts training the child. She teaches the baby either to suck the bottle or mother. The training continues. The child learns where and when to pass faeces, what to eat, what to put on, etc. It goes on further. He learns the language, how to address mother, father, guests, seniors, etc. This process of learning goes on and he becomes a person by learning the social manners, social customs, morals, laws, etc. He, as a member of the society, tries to establish his place in his group---family, neighbourhood, village, etc.

So, he does not remain a mere organism but becomes a person through the process of socialisation. What he is today, is the product of interaction of the organism with psychological, social and geographical factors. And, the social functioning (how does he act in relation to self and others) is the result of the interaction of man, who is a product of biological (physical), psychological (thinking, feeling, perception, learning, memory, etc.) and social (membership of the group which has its own norms, values, customs and a certain style of living) factors, with the environmental factors like the human beings, the living bodies, the climate, the amenities of life and the natural surroundings, etc.

In the psycho-social study and diagnosis, efforts are made to locate the bio-psycho-social factors *vis-à-vis* environmental factors and understand their contribution to the social functioning and the problem of the client.

(2) *All problems in social functioning are psycho-social in nature and most are interpersonal as well.* Social casework, to start with was more concerned with socio-psychological problems. With the advancement in the field, social casework has been described as a psychological process also dealing with psycho-social problems as well.

The fact is that no unit of our functioning in the society, say any act, is either purely psychological or social. It may originate in 'psyche' and get expressed in social (psycho-social) or it may originate in 'social' and get expressed through psyche (socio-psychological). For example, I think to present a pen to my child and I give it. This is psychosocial in nature. Similarly, when I see my teacher, I bow down and greet him, which is termed as a socio-psychological act. However, in all the acts, we see both social as well as psychological components. Thinking takes place in a social context, and the way I think, has been patterned by the society. Our ideas, beliefs and attitudes have been learnt from the society and its culture.

All the problems caseworkers deal with are psycho-social in nature, i.e., they have psychological as well as social components. (Here, psycho-social is used in terms of psychological and social and not in terms of which precedes the other one, as mentioned in the earlier paragraph). The causative factors of the problem may be either in the psyche or in the social circumstances or in their interaction (Gestalt). Many a time, these problems have interpersonal components as well.

So, during the exploratory and diagnostic process one tries to understand the characteristic way of functioning, interaction of the psyche and social forces, and relationship pattern of the client.

(3) *Within certain limits, man can be understood and helped.* Man is, as discussed earlier, a product of a very subtle and complicated interaction process between bio-psycho-social (including environmental) factors. Under no circumstances any one can understand this process to the fullest extent. Nobody can remember all that has happened to him during his earlier parts of life. This becomes more evident when we find that one invariably forgets what has happened to him even during one day. This is the human limitation.

Hence, naturally, one can study and understand a person within certain limits only and thus the help to be given to him will be limited by the understanding of the man in question and the availability of various resources.

The diagnostic formulations should outline these limitations in evaluation of the 'person-in-situation' as well as the help to be extended to him.

(4) *Man can grow and change limited only by his inherent capacities and potentials.* This assumption implies that there is no limit to growth and development of an individual except the one imposed by our genetic potentialities inherited by us. For example, we cannot make a person with an I.Q. of 50 compete with a person of 100 I.Q. This assumption helps us plan our intervention realistically and reduces our frustration involved in the process of helping others.

(5) *Every person is unique as well as similar to others.* (See principle of individualisation for its explanation).

Principles

Principles are certain assertions or statements which guide our professional action. In social casework practice, these principles are as discussed under:

Principle of Acceptance

Acceptance implies liking the client irrespective of his negative qualities and conduct. It is an expression of goodwill towards the client and criticisms (evaluation) if any are done out of goodwill. It is conveying deep concern and active understanding to the client who is liked by the worker in spite of his problem—behaviour for which he is hated or punished by the society. No effective relationship is possible without accepting the client. Unless we really accept the client, we cannot work out his problems. When disliked by us, we may behave to keep him off from ourselves and no positive relationship (report) will be possible. Acceptance involves observance of common courtesies and respect for his ideas and treating him as equal to self; for example, leaving chair, wishing him, moving forward to receive, or see him off, respecting appointments, etc., are indicators of acceptance (see acceptance in chapter on 'Relationship').

Principle of Confidentiality

Everyone prefers to keep his things to himself and saves it from leaking out unless its divulge is more beneficial to the person. Once the worker imbibes the value of worth and dignity of an individual, he will refrain from encroaching upon the client's privacy, and maintain the confidence reposed in him. Once the client loses confidence in him, he will not believe the worker and the whole process of communication will break down, and impossible will be the task to assist the helpee in his problems or in fulfilment of his needs. Maintaining confidentiality for all the transactions, that take place between the caseworker and client in correctional settings or other places where law needs information for justice purpose, is very difficult or impossible. In all such situations, the client must be made aware of these limitations. Concept of confidentiality in western society is much different than what it is in India. In our country, wife and husband have minimum things to hide from each other as compared to their counterparts in the western, specially American, society. In majority of Indian families wives cannot be interviewed without explicit permission of the husband or in-laws. Its roots lie in our cultural beliefs and values (like seven vows taken during the Hindu marriage), norms and systems like joint family etc. Our society is more group-oriented as compared to individual-oriented western society. Our society's group orientation emphasises on one's duty to others around us. It is these factors that limit the use of principles of confidentiality in our practice. These limits are true of Mohammdens and Christians also as they too equally share these Indian norms, values and beliefs.

Principle of Relationship (Rapport)

According to this principle, relationship is the medium to help anyone. Relationship has to be positive to be effective. No relationship, no communication. Relationship is an emotional bond, which works as a transmitting belt between the concerned parties. No rapport, no help (see the chapter on 'Relationships'). Relationship (positive) is the basis of all help. In relationship, feelings play an important role, therefore, these need to be understood and handled properly.

Principle of Resource Utilisation

This principle is based on the value that the society has responsibility to provide necessary facilities for self-actualisation of its members. Services are provided to the individual in recognition of his contributions to the society. It is only because of this that the government takes care of those who are not cared for by anyone, e.g., orphans, destitute, handicapped, etc. Therefore, all the personal resources and resources available within the community, agency and with the relatives of the client should be utilised to help the client. Resources may be in terms of money, material, power and influence, talents and capabilities etc.

Principle of Right of Self-determination

This principle is based on a very fundamental democratic value. According to this, everyone has the right to govern his life as he wishes provided it does not interfere with others' right to govern their lives. Right of self-determination has been demanded by various people living in various regions of the world so that they can choose their own government. Caseworkers have to give this right to the client so that he can decide and take best possible action in his self-interest. This is reasonable also because he knows himself better than others. And, the caseworker is only an enabler who helps him through his expertise to take the best possible decision and action in the circumstances.

The caseworkers should understand that this right is limited and is a relative and not an absolute one. There are clients who are unable to take proper decisions about self, e.g., children, immature adults, the psychotics and the retarded, and they should not be given this right except to harm themselves.

Principle of Self-awareness

This principle has emerged from the experience of practitioners who have observed and experienced that social work practitioners substitute their personal values, norms, etc., for professional values and norms while assisting their clients. They have been observed as projecting their own feelings and imposing their values and norms on them. All these simply destroy the helping process. In fact, the worker should

(i) be aware of and work through his own coercive and moralistic attitude, personal values and norms etc.;
(ii) be conscious of and accept his own feelings of aggression, love or gratitude or such other feelings;
(iii) examine his own motivation to save, punish or deprive the client; and
(iv) avoid projection of his own family relationships to the client's family situation.

Self-awareness helps the caseworkers to use only professional values and norms and help the client in such a way that he is able to re-live comfortably when he goes back to his own society. Self-awareness also helps the workers to be objective and non-judgemental (avoid "assigning guilt, innocense or degree of client responsibility for causation of the problems or needs") in his approach.

Principle of Purposiveness of Behaviour

Every behaviour is functional and serves useful purpose even though it may not serve or fulfil a person's conscious or deliberate design. Behaviour includes all expressions of our body—verbal as well as non-verbal. Hence, all the relevant behaviours (except reflex actions) expressed during the casework interviews, or other ones known to have been indulged in by the client in other situations, should be analysed and assessed (diagnosed) to plan a realistic approach to help the client to replace his inappropriate behaviour with an appropriate one and to critically examine the purpose behind his problem behaviour or behaviour pattern. Assessment of these behaviours of the client speaks either about the personality of the client or his situation or about the nature of their interaction.

Principle of Requirements of Agency Practice and Settings

Every caseworker, to avoid frustration to himself and the client and to be effective in his services, should know the policies and procedures of the agency thoroughly. He must know the limitations of the agency as well as that of the setting in which the agency is operating. Settings like psychiatric or correctional or family welfare etc. pose their own problems because of their inherent nature. Do's and don'ts, material resources, nature of services, legal requirements and sanctions, etc., are to be properly utilised for the benefit of the client. Agency limitations should be fully explained to the client to be effective.

Principle of Beginning where the Client is

This principle appears to have been derived from Gestalt therapy. The principle directs to know what the client is experiencing, what he wants and what he feels at this moment. His feelings are as important as any other objective fact. Knowing these may clear the deck for further work or give important clues to deal effectively with the client's problems. The worker should start his interview "with the concern of person or with their felt needs" (Johnson, 1983).

Principle of Individualisation

We know that every person is similar to others as well as unique in himself. This assumption becomes clear when we notice that the theories of psychology, sociology, medicine, etc., apply to all the persons because everyone possesses the common characterisations of a man. At the same time, he has certain characteristics which are unique to him only. This uniqueness comes to him because of differing background of every individual and because of many minute and subtle psychological and constitutional differences. Inter-play between bio-psycho-social factors and environment gives a certain shape to personality which is unique to the person though he is similar to others because he has human figure, thinking capacity and feelings like any other human being.

It is because of this assumption only that we have to identify the special ways of the client behaving in social situations and the special help he needs. This principle of individualisation stipulates that the social caseworker will relate and help every client as an individual who is unique and whose problems and needs are special to him. For example, everyone seeks a job, but what job, with what salary, where, what sort of boss and what perks etc. are the unique requirements of each individual.

Similarly, the situation of the client, his problems of social functioning, his dominant mode of adjustment and the lifestyle, his ego-strength etc. are unique; therefore, the caseworker should probe these areas specifically in each case. While helping, one should select modes of helping (techniques) according to the intellectual level, socio-economic situation, ego-strength, etc., of the client. Thus individualisation reminds one to pay attention to the specific needs, problems, situations and resources and capacities of each client.

Social casework involves helping individuals with their problems in social functioning through a systematic approach. Knowledge of human behaviour and social situation and skills in human relationship is basic to its practice. It is an art when it uses various ways to effect change in human behaviour and a science when it uses knowledge of human behaviour and social situations. Social casework can thus be said to be scientific art to help an individual to live a socially productive and individually satisfying life limited to by his capacities and social realities.

Trends

In the 1980s, the trends appear to be (1) greater use of interventive approaches, results of which can be measured and standardised; (2) increasing use of various concepts from various theories and disciplines; (3) emphasis on coping skills with less focus on the inner problems; (4) blending of different casework models of practice for better results; (5) integrated (unitary) approach.

The different models currently in practice are discussed as under:

Psycho-social Model

This incorporates psycho-analytical concepts and principles and uses ego psychology with concepts from other behavioural sciences and understands behaviour in terms of cause and effect. Gordon Hamilton, Florence Hollis and Lucille Austin are the advocates of this model.

Functional Model

Developed at Pennsylvania School of Social Work (USA), this model has important contributions from Jessie Taft and Virginia Robinson. This is based on the concept of relationship, dynamic use of time, and "use of agency" functions. Otto Rank's psychological concept of 'will' is used. Diagnostic categorisation is avoided (see details in Chapter 8).

Problem-solving Model

Identified with the work of Perlman (1957), this model involves (i) identification of the problem by the person, (ii) assessment of subjective aspects of the person-in-the-situation and centrality of the person with the problem, (iii) search for solutions, (iv) decision-making, and (v) action. The process is to free the person for investment in tasks related to the solution of the problem, involve the client's ego in efforts to deal with the problem and to mobilise personal and social forces and resources for satisfactory role performance.

Behaviour Modification Model

Based on the work of Pavlov, Thorndike, Skinners, Wolpe, Eysenck and Gantt, this model is very much advocated by Edwin J. Thomas of Michigan University. In this approach, experimental research is very much feasible as behaviour modification is observable. According to it, problem behaviour is learned and it obeys the same laws of learning and conditioning as it is in the case of normal behaviour. Behaviour can be de-learned, re-learned and modified to the extent desirable (see Chapter 3 for details).

Task-centered Model

It is a promising general service model or social casework developed by William Reid at Chicago University and cannot be said to be school of thought like the earlier ones. According to Reid (1978), it is "short-term, time-limited form or practice designed to help individuals and families with specific psycho-social problems. The practitioner and client are expected to reach on explicit agreement on the particular problem to be dealt with and on the probable duration of service (eight to twelve sessions)".

Work on the client's problems is organised about tasks or problem-solving actions that the client and caseworker develop collaboratively. A task may state general direction for the client's action, such as to improve his work performance or it may specify a particular behaviour the client is to undertake, such as to telephone his wife if he is going to be home late. The caseworker concentrates his efforts on helping clients carry out these tasks. In doing so, he makes use of an eclectic combination of interventions from insight development to dispensation of tangible reinforces (see Chapter 8 for details).

Though difficult to classify problems, some attempts have been made to re-group the problems social caseworkers deal with. One such effort to classify problems is: (a) environmental and sociological, (b) interpersonal and familial, and (c) personal and intrapsychic. Boehm (1959) comments on the current state of classification of problems in social casework. According to him, (1) problems to which casework is addressed are conceived in terms of both the psychic and the social factors which affect a person's social functioning; (2) casework problem's categories which are needed for effective diagnosis have not been developed to any large extent but the field or practice seems to be moving in this direction; (3) conceptualisation of the phenomenon of practice will facilitate the research needed to establish problem categories; and (4) the term 'problem' is not clearly defined and is frequently used synonymously with stress. Stress is a pressure which may manifest itself in malfuctioning. Malfunctioning is the problem.

Social Casework and Indian Social Condition

When we look at the Indian scenario, we find it beset with poverty, diseases and ignorance. According to official sources,

48 percent (51.2 percent in rural) people were below poverty line in 1977-78, and 36.9 percent (40.4 percent in rural) continued to exist below this line in 1983-84, though non-official estimates put this figure around 59 percent. Jay Dubashi (1986) has also questioned the official statistics. Unemployment in 1987 was reported to be 9.2 million as against unofficial estimates of 26 million (TV-Focus Programme, 17 January 1988). The gap between the rich and the poor has also widened. The top 30 percent own 80 percent of the national assets against only 2 percent owned by the bottom 30 percent in 1986, while their share was 2.5 percent in 1960-61. Likewise the top 5 percent income earners have 22 percent of the national income while bottom 40 percent have less than 16 percent of the same. In the rural areas, the top 4 percent own 30 percent of the total assets while bottom 20 percent had hardly 1 percent of the assets (Laharia, 1986). The per capital gross national income remained at Rs. 2,550 in 1984-85 according to the government statistics.

During 1986 and 1987 starvation deaths were reported in Kalahandi district of Orissa. This is because economic, social and political power is concentrated in a few hands, the benefits of developmental works are enjoyed by a few, and the benefits of developmental programmes have percolated to the poor to a very limited extent. Political will and administrative capacity "to remove poverty have been missing". Corruption is rampant in our country: the poor have to bribe various people including bank and state government officials (Jammu, 1986) for securing loan under various government programmes and schemes.

On the health front, clean and safe drinking water is available to only 31 percent of the rural masses, who form more than 70 percent of the Indian population. Mortality rate in 1987 was 105 per 1,000 live births. Malnutrition, communicable diseases, etc., are yet to be brought under control. Population continued to increase at the rate of 32.7 percent in 1986 as per census records. Literacy rate is at 36.20 percent according to

1981 census. Communal riots, casteism, regionalism, etc., are the worst enemy of the vulnerable masses constituting about 80 percent of our population. Though India has been declared as a sovereign republic, it continues to be ruled mainly by a nexus of "politicians and big businessmen" (*Hindustan Times*, 2 February, 1988).

It is only because of these appalling conditions that radical social workers are seeking change in the existing values, societal conditions and social system. Leonard (1975) talks of "building of counter system either within or outside the existing system". Case Con, an organisation of social workers in the UK, is seeking replacement of present state with a "worker's state, based on the interests of the vast majority of population".

Can social casework, in such socio-economic conditions of India, be useful to render services to the people? The answer cannot be 'no' simply because (i) there is population, may be small in proportion, which needs help to solve their problems at individual level, (ii) there are problems like sickness, feuds, interpersonal conflicts, etc., which can be dealt with only at individual level, and (iii) people need curative and rehabilitative services also, though developmental services are more needed in our Indian conditions. Social caseworkers will have to emphasise 'indirect' casework services (Richmond, 1917) and create a congenial atmosphere for those seeking self-actualisation. Bisno (1952) has also opined that casework and social action are complementary to each other, and that casework should continue to serve the needy population.

How Casework Works

During the casework sessions, clients talk about their problems and related past, present and future. Caseworkers pick up points where problems have arisen because of lack of information, knowledge and misperception of the situation. The experiences (misperceptions, feelings and reactions) are corrected in and through the discussions. Emphasis should be given on the discussion of day-to-day behaviour of the client in relation to his problem and in doing so, correct his misperceptions which may be unrealistic because of emotions, past incidents, unrealistic future expectations or unsuitable lifestyle etc. (various reasons and means for correction and modification of these have been discussed in the chapter on 'Treatment Process'). Once the therapist starts taking care of these points in day-to-day life of the client, he slowly starts perceiving and changing his ways of behaving.

Apart from this, talking alone helps in many ways. It helps in ventilating one's feelings and thus frees one from the pressure of these feelings. Talking to an expert is in itself quite reassuring. Talking by itself in many cases results in insight into one's behaviour, thus equipping one with better ways or managing the life affairs.

It is through these processes only that the client substitutes his unrealistic and irrational beliefs and definitions by realistic and correct ones, straightens his attitudes, develops self-control over his feelings, and changes his lifestyle necessary to achieve what he desires to achieve in life. Material resources are used as tools to effect desirable changes in his situation and functioning.

Social Casework in Layman's Language

It is sometimes difficult to explain the nature of social casework, i.e., how does it help the client (the one seeking help) to layman. In this section an attempt is made to describe social casework process in non-technical terms.

We all know that man continues to grow and tries to shape himself as he wishes. In the process of growing, he develops certain attitudes, beliefs, ideas and ways of reacting and expressing feelings etc. in different situations. At certain points of life, he fails to deal with the situation confronting him, and he then turns towards his social circle (friends, parents, priests and teachers etc.) for help in dealing with the situation. At times, his social circle fails to solve his problems. In such a situation one seeks expert help to deal with these situations. Experts are available in different areas of life (medical, legal, business, social, sexual) who are trained and experienced in helping people in their area of operation.

The experts in social life, i.e., trained social workers, help individuals, groups, communities through various methods of social work known as social casework, social group work, and community organisation. A social caseworker, when someone comes to him for help in dealing with his situation, tries to know and locate (study) various possible factors (including people) responsible for creating the problem-situation and blocking its solution. His knowledge of human behaviour (achieved through study of various subjects like psychology, sociology, health and illness, etc.) helps in finding out these factors easily. In collecting informations on these aspects, he talks to the client, his family, friends, relatives or employer and consults records wherever important to understand the problem-situation. These factors lie either in the nature of person, his way of dealing with or in the situation of the person. Caseworker (therapist) also collects informations about the resources of the person. Resources mean capacities of the person, his social contacts, and his financial and material possessions. In the second phase, he shares and discusses his understanding of and plans to manage or tackle the problem with the client (diagnosis and treatment planning).

Help is rendered either through discussion or providing with some service, material or financial resources wherever available and required. The discussion or talk is conducted in a particular way. Talking equips the needy person to gain confidence, knowledge and information necessary to deal with the situation. It also helps the persons to see how emotions lead to misperception or block perceiving the reality (example can be given), to understand his own role in creating the problem-situation, to evaluate and understand his ways of taking decision and resultant consequences, and how his beliefs are unrealistic, how his childhood feelings and attitudes are affecting his (client's) behaviour with the people in his current situation etc. The caseworker can help the client to formulate his family budget, schooling of children, etc., according to the principles of economics and education. He can guide and advise him in certain situations. If need be, talking (interview) sessions are also conducted with persons (like parents, teachers, spouse, etc.) important for solution of the client's problem-situation.

Social caseworker, thus, helps the client to understand his self, his situation and his ways of deciding and acting to enable him to modify (or enrich) his style of thinking, feeling and acting and to solve his immediate and future problems.

3

Concepts and Theoretical Approaches

It is now very much agreed that "there is need for a variety of conceptual frames and theories to embrace the richness of behaviour". Psycho-social behaviour, the subject matter of social work, can be understood only in terms of various behavioural and social science concepts, constructs and hypotheses. The social worker should, therefore, acquaint himself with salient materials in sociology, psychology, psycho-analysis, philosophy and other cognate disciplines before he undertakes cases to deal with.

Some of the most (alongwith suggestions to use some other) used concepts and constructs are briefly discussed in this chapter. However, the readers are suggested to refer to the relevant materials to have better and comprehensive understanding of these concepts.

Psycho-analysis

Social casework practice is most influenced by psycho-analytical thinking and concepts. Psycho-analysis, a school of psychology, advocates psychic determinism, therefore understands human behaviour in terms of unconscious factors and instinctual forces. Instinct, in simple words, is an inborn tendency to behave in a particular way. It is an inborn capacity too. Personality and its functioning is understood by psycho-analysts from mainly two types of concepts—topographic and structural.

Topographic

According to this, any mental event is either conscious, pre-conscious or unconscious. The unconscious is a dynamic (always interacting and in action) body of wishes which are repressed because of the anxiety these generate. Man, while awake, thinks many things but does not act on all of them as these are socially non-acceptable. All such wishes, therefore, are forgotten by one, i.e., they get stored in the unconscious part of the mind. Thus, unconscious consists of a variety of wishes which continue to press for discharge. These wishes originate because of our instinctual needs (like sex, hunger, etc.) and the related matters. These wishes when socially unacceptable get outlet only in dreams, fantasies and psychotic behaviours etc. An analysis of these aspects can help us to know the nature of unconscious. Slips of tongue or pen etc. are also analysed to know the pressing contents of unconscious. An idea, which is irrational and non-acceptable at conscious level, is ruled by the primary process whose main characteristic is to strive for immediate discharge either through fantasies or dreams etc. Primary process is responsible for symbolisation, i.e., many unconscious materials, to be acceptable, are represented in conscious life through symbols. Symbol is used by the primary process to conceal the true meaning of the details or unconscious life materials. Contrary to primary is the secondary process which operates in the conscious part and is socially acceptable and rational. Secondary process is dominated by reality principle in contrast to primary process which is ruled by pleasure principle. Pre-conscious consists of usually those events which can be recollected with a bit of effort. Unconscious materials are recalled only through special techniques like free association, hypno-analysis etc., for which one has to be trained in psycho-analysis.

Structural

Apart from unconscious factors, one should, according to psycho-analysis, study the dynamic forces also. To understand these forces in operation, personality functioning is understood in terms of id, ego and superego. Id is the source (store) of all drives (sex, hunger, thirst, excretion) and instinctual energy. All our urges and impulses are part of id. One gets pleasure by getting immediate gratification of these urges (sexual and aggressive). Immediate gratification or gratification even at a later stage (of the urges) is not always feasible because of social realities (conditions). However, when id is denied gratification to the extent that these urges pile up there is always a danger that these impulses may force their way through the ego (conscious force) resulting in breakdown of the personality. This sort of breakdown is seen in patients suffering from psychosis.

Ego is considered to be the chief executive of the personality and a balancing force between id and superego. The force which keeps the id impulses, wishes and instinctual drives in check as an adaptive measure to the pressure of the outside world, is termed as ego. It acts in the services of id (instincts) by modifying, inhibiting and seeking outlets for them in accordance with external reality. Thus ego directs and balances activities among id, superego and external reality through negotiation. Freud (1964) explains that ego owes its origin as well as the most important of its acquired characteristics to its relation to the real world. I think ego takes a clear form once the infant begins to perceive his body as distinct from the external world. This perception is strengthened by fondling of the infant by various persons and stimulating him to respond to their gestures, and calling him by various nick names, i.e., recognising his identity. In casework practice, appraisal of functions of ego, specially the defense mechanisms, serves the purpose of understanding the person's social functioning and his role in creation of the problems he brings to the workers for solution.

Defense Mechanisms

A person, according to psycho-analysis, is normal when he (ego) is able to handle the demands of id, superego and reality effectively and without conflict. Demands of reality or of id (instinctual drives) pose threat to ego. External threats (real ones) are easily handled by ego, but the danger (threat) from within is difficult to handle. Whenever ego senses that acting on an impulse or even just experiencing it will create danger or perceives or interprets a situation or stimuli as dangerous, it creates anxiety. *Anxiety* is a signal of impending danger (external or internal). If a person interprets a situation as threatening and is able to cope with stressor, i.e., situation or stimuli, he may resort to intrapsychic manoeuvres (defense mechanisms) to eliminate anxiety state. When any sexual wish or aggressive desire (i.e., instinctual drive) gets activated and when these are against the superego (ethical norms) or reality of the situation, defenses prohibit experiencing these impulses and ward off the anxiety. Ego defends itself from the anxiety resulting from the threat of the impulse seeking immediate gratification. Anxiety is always associated with the threats to ego either from instinctual drives or outside force and defense mechanism modifies, distorts or renders unconscious the feelings, thoughts, memories that would otherwise provoke anxiety.

Freud and his daughter, Anna Freud have enumerated various defense mechanisms. These can be observed in the behaviour of an individual and are not restricted to any part of life. These are operative at unconscious level only. In brief, defense mechanisms are regarded as innate coping styles which allow individuals to minimise sudden, often unexpected, changes in internal and external environment and to resolve cognitive dissonance (psychological conflicts). They are unconscious coping styles. They help in managing instincts and affects, are unconscious, dynamic and reversible and are usually adaptive, not pathological, in process. These defense mechanisms are described as under:

Repression

The sexual and aggressive desires and other related materials not acceptable to ego at conscious level are pushed into unconscious where these desires remain active and try to intrude into the awareness of ego. Ego represses these because it does not want to be aware of the actual situation (desires, ideas and impulses). Ego has to spend a lot of psychic energy in prohibiting the repressed material (idea or feeling) from coming into consciousness. These ideas or feelings are forgotten only to the extent that the ego has expelled it or withheld from consciousness. These ideas, feelings and desires may get expressed in dreams.

Denial

Seeing (perceiving) but refusing to accept what one sees, is denial. Often students poor at study, think of getting 1st division, explains denial of what one knows. The unpleasant reality is not accepted by the person as it poses a threat to him; therefore, he denies it, and thus wards off the anxiety created by this threat.

Reaction Formation

This mechanism helps the patient/client to develop feelings/attitudes opposite to the anxiety provoking attitudes/feelings. Unacceptable impulses are expressed in antithetical form. A mother who hates to have a child starts loving the child too much if she happens to have one. Similarly, adolescents who experience anxiety because they are criticised for being afraid, dependent and cooperative, turn out to be independent, self-confident and defiant.

Isolation

This occurs when ego, to avoid anxiety, isolates feelings from thoughts or vice versa. This is seen when one describes full details of the accidental death of his friend without feeling the sad feelings associated with the narration of the incident. It involves separation of affect from the content (thoughts) through repression of either affect or idea.

Projection

Desires, impulses and feelings unacceptable to the individual are attributed to someone in his milieu. He is afraid of accepting these impulses etc. as they create anxiety in him; consequently he ascribes these to others and accuses them of having these impulses and desires. For example, when he feels hostility towards some, he may repress it and tell that some people are hostile to him. The individual says, in effect, that "it is not I who have thought or wished. It is other who does". In simple words, it is accusing others of having the impulses and desires that the client himself possesses. This is usually seen in the patients of Paranoid State.

Regression

When one fails to adopt to reality, he may return to an earlier stage of functioning, i.e., he will regress (as opposed to progression) from his present stage of social functioning. An adolescent unable to cope up with college life may regress to pre-school age in his behaviour. Similarly, a child in genital stage may regress to anal period and start wetting the bed when confronted with hard reality. It is a return to a previous stage of development, re-enacting behaviour that was given up, to avoid anxieties involved in the current stage of development or later (one to follow the current) stage of development.

Introjection

Identification and introjection are virtually same in nature. Introjection is seen when we internalise (as opposed to projection) the characteristics of the object with the aim of establishing closeness to the object. Superego is built by introjection, i.e., taking in or introjecting moral and ethical standards (values, norms etc.) of the parents. Identification is also defined in the same way, i.e., as a process of associating and affiliating with someone, that is, his values, standards and behaviour patterns are incorporated into self. Freud illustrates identification by the example that a child who feels small and inadequate, reduces the consequent anxiety by identifying with the parent of the opposite sex, who is seen by the child as strong and competent in the world. A child deprived of satisfactory adult model to introject or identify with (e.g., father, uncle, elder brother, etc., in home) is likely to be more frustrated in his growing up because he will always realise his failures and will not be able to repress/rationalise his failures.

Displacement

It occurs when a person expresses his feelings or impulses on a person or object other than the object/person who stimulates the feelings. An officer angry with his boss may bang his peon; or a washerman when angry with his customer starts hitting his animal, thus, displacing his anger from customer to the animal (see transference also).

Sublimation

Socially and personally unacceptable impulses (aggressive or sexual) seek expression at conscious level. Since these are denied expression because of social implications, psychic energy associated with these impulses may produce tension and anxiety. A mature way, then, is to channel these instinctual drives. Detouring of this energy is sublimation in which the aim or object is changed from a socially objectionable one to a socially acceptable one. Aggressive impulses get sublimated in pleasurable games and sports, hunting etc., and the sexual impulses get expression into artistic, literary or scientific activities. Saint Tulsidas is a classical example of sublimation of sexual instincts. His (sexual) impulses got sublimated into socially valued activity (study of Vedic literature and writing books etc.). Sublimation along with repression, reaction formation plays a very important role in formation of character.

Suppression

It is similar to repression except in one aspect, i.e., the conscious impulse or conflict is deliberately and knowingly pushed aside. This is a mature defense as it involves proper perception and realistic decision. It is a semi-conscious effort to control and inhibit an unacceptable impulse, idea or emotion. Repression is an unconscious process.

Rationalisation

Whenever we are questioned to explain our attitudes, beliefs or behaviour unacceptable to others, anxiety overhelms us. In such situations we rationalise the attitudes etc., or, in other words, give rational arguments to justify it. Reasons given are plausible-sounding though the real reasons remain repressed. This is done at unconscious level. Any argument given knowingly and consciously to justify one's action is not rationalisation but an excuse. Rationalisation is very commonly used.

Intellectualisation

Herein logic or reasoning (much more systematic than in rationalisation) is used to avoid confrontation with an objectionable impulse or affect. Impulses or affects are controlled by thinking (intellectual efforts) about them, whereas in rationalisation, one gives convincing arguments for his failure like a student who explains reasons for his failure in examination.

Compensation

We, many times, accept a substitute goal or activity that gives partial satisfaction when we fail to satisfy our motives directly.

Example can be quoted of a student poor at studies trying to earn medals in sports or cultural or political activities or in other aspects of social life. He, thus, compensates for his deficiencies in studies.

To support ego, defense mechanisms like suppression, sublimation, reaction formation, etc., are strengthened and supported in social casework situations (see 'Treatment Process' in Chapter 8).

Appraisal of Ego Functions

The appraisal of different functions of ego will serve as a practical guide to assess strength, weaknesses, and the clients' accessibility for treatment. Some of the most important functions are narrated as follows:

Object Relationship

The content of the social study data (both historical and current) as well as the therapist's observations in the interview with the client, will give us an idea about the degree to which the client's libidinal resources (psychic energy, a life urge) are invested in self and how much remains free to be used for investment in others for warm and empathic relationships with them. The worker must focus his observations on the client's ability to be "in touch" with the world around him. Lack of genuine contact or ability to sustain contact during the interview will give a clue to the worker as to the nature of emotional attachment to the client with others. Also, a careful knowledge of the client's extent and depth of contacts with other people in his past and current life situation will enhance the diagnostic picture.

Reality Testing

This function of the ego permits a person to distinguish between actual objects and situations and his fantasies. It consists of objective evaluation and judgement of the world outside the self. The proper assessment of this function (capacity to function according to social and physical realities) gives us clues to the degree and extent of pathology involved.

Judgement

This is a function closely related to reality testing and involves the power of the person's ability to deduce correct impressions from the experiences in the past and apply the deductions to current situations. This function aids planning, and, when it is adequate, enables the person to know what is appropriate and what is not, in relation to other people. In effect, he learns from past experiences, sees cause and effect, learns from his own mistakes and foresees the consequences of his activities.

Motility Patterns

Evaluation of this function involves assessing the physical coordination and the range of activity or inactivity with which individual meets life situations and pursues his goals and purposes in daily life. In evaluating this function, the worker must consider the client's activities or inactivities in relation to both inside pressures and the stimuli from outside.

Tolerance for Frustrations

There is an overlapping of this function with that of judgement and morality patterns. Tolerance for frustration obviously involves the ability to postpone the need for immediate gratifications. Consideration must also be given to the cost of gratification postponement to the ego and its functioning ability.

Perception

Clinically defined, this function of the ego permits receiving and interpreting stimuli from the outside world. This function overlaps with reality testing and, if adequate, it helps the client to sort out stimuli, both physical and emotional in nature, and to make choice. Perception involves knowing the reality---physical and social---around us.

Affectivity

To assess the degree of the client's affect, its range, adequacy and appropriateness is an important task for the worker. Some clients are unable to experience genuine emotions and/or show indications of mood disturbances. In assessing this function, the worker must be particularly attuned to the signs of pervasive (lasting for longer periods) moods since these offer clues to pathological states.

Defense Mechanisms

In the normal course of human growth, certain defense mechanisms are developed by ego against anxiety which are used by the person in various situations and become characteristic ways of coping. In working with the client, the worker must be constantly alert to repetitive behaviour responses. These defense mechanisms, like repression, projection, reaction formation, etc., are always unconscious.

Basic Intellectual Capacities

The worker must attempt to determine the client's basic potential and inherent capacities to make profitable use of his experiences and endowments. In situations where emotional difficulties interfere, there is a discrepancy between the client's functioning and his potential; in other words, the person is unable to function according to his capabilities.

Adaptation and Reality

Assessment of the adaptive patterns of the ego to the environment is an important task for the worker in the diagnostic process. Does it use flight, fight or compromise to cope up with the situation or is it flexible in its approach? These questions must be answered.

Organising Function

This function of ego includes both the synthesising function and differentiation so that the person is able to think, feel and act in an organised and directed manner. It can be considered only in conjunction with all the other functions. It is the ego's tendency to unite, organise and bind together various drives, tendencies and functions which go alongwith the tendency to simplify and generalise ideas about various situations.

Superego can be defined "in terms of attitudes". It is seen when the individual expresses his morals and observes socially approved behavioural norms. It is censor of the mind and contains do's and don'ts. The social norms expressed in the behaviour of parents are internalised by the child around the end of pre-oedipal period. These social pressures become demands which we make upon ourselves even when there is no longer any outside pressure. It includes what is known popularly as conscience (internalised controls and limits which forbids and admonishes), and ego-ideal, the definition of acceptable goals, values, morals to itself.

Apart from these two (topographic and structural) views psycho-analysis takes *dynamic*, *economic* and *genetic* views also into consideration to understand personality and human behaviour. The dynamic view is concerned with the interaction of libidinal and aggressive drives. This view helps assess motivation and capacity for working with the therapists. The economic view tries to study the quantity and quality of the psychic energy (libido, i.e., life urge, and aggression) invested in behaviour. Genetic postulates view human behaviour in the light of the significance of issues and events in the individual's past which lead upto current behaviour. The concept of *transference* is related to this genetic postulate when the individual brings into his new relationship (e.g., with caseworker) the "irrational elements" carried over from past meaningful relationship (like that with parents, sibs etc.).

Transference

We, thus, bring unconscious apart from conscious, feelings and attitudes in our current important relationships. These unconscious attitudes and associated feelings transferred from the past onto the present relationship considered as transferences are irrational. The person or client transfers these into the present interaction because of some similarity of the actors in the current situation with those he has encountered earlier in life (i.e., childhood). In other words, the individual relates with the person in the current situation (e.g., worker, boss, etc.) as if he is the one of his earlier life situations and does not relate with him as he really is. To quote Dewald (cited in Singh, 1968), transference is "a form of displacement in which the individual unconsciously displaces onto a current object those drives, defenses, attitudes, feelings, and responses which were experienced or developed in relationship with earlier objects (mainly persons) in the individual's life. Since the prototypes of all object relationships are the earliest relationship to parents, these serve as the core and origin of the psychic experiences transferred to the current objects. This displacement occurs unconsciously and thereby leads the individual to experience reactions towards the current object which are derived not from the reality of the present situation and interaction, but rather from his own unconscious internal psychic life." It may be positive (love, liking, etc.) or negative (irrational, hostile feelings) in nature. It is related to the concepts of regression, displacement and the repetition compulsion. Displacement is one of the defense mechanisms in which one transfers his/her feelings from the object in the current situation to another one in the current situation itself but the feelings in transference are displaced from one in the past to the one in current and *not* from one in the current to another object in the current situation. Transference is tackled by clarification (clarifying the reality), interpretation, spacing the interview, etc.

Stages of Development

Erikson (1950) believes that personality continues to be moulded throughout the entire lifespan from birth to death. This period has been divided into eight stages by him. Each stage has its characteristic features marked and affected by emotional crisis, particular culture of the person and his interaction with the society of which he is a part.

Oral Stage

This stage expands from zero to one-and-a-half years. During this period mouth is the sensitive zone of the body and the main source of joy and pleasure for the child. How the infant is being cared for by the mother makes the infant trust or mistrust the world (represented by mother) around him. If his wants are frequently satisfied, he develops trust and believes that the world will take care of him. In case of frequent dissatisfaction, mistrust develops leading the infant to believe that the people around him cannot be believed, relied on, and that he is going to lose most of what he wants. After the first six months (sucking period), the remaining one year (biting period) is fairly difficult for the child and mother because of eruption of teeth and weaning. If properly handled, infant's trust gets reinforced and he develops an in-built and lifelong spring of optimism and hope.

Persons, who had an unpleasant (abandoned, unloved and uncared) babyhood, are likely to find parenthood as burdensome and may express dependent, helpless, abusive behaviour, and angry outbursts i.e., oral character. To such people, caseworker is like parents, who helps the client to verbalise his anger and distrust and later provides emotional support and protective services. The caseworker has to fill the voids (mistrust) created by the early mother and child relationship. The caseworker presents himself as a trustworthy person, and, as a by-product of this relationship the client starts trusting himself and others, around him. Care should be taken that the client does not feel deprived at the hands of the caseworker who presents himself as a mothering person to the client. It may be made clear that the feeling of trust or mistrust (task of oral stage) is not totally dependent upon mother-child relationship during oral stage. It continues to be modified, reinforced or impoverished according to the experiences of the client in the subsequent years of life also.

Anal Stage

Towards the end of biting period of oral stage, the child is able to walk, talk, and eat on his own. He can retain or release something that he has. This is true of bowel and bladder function also. He can either retain or release his bowel and bladder contents. Now, the child no more depends upon the mouth zone for pleasure. He now derives pleasure from bowel and bladder (anal zone) functioning, which entails anxiety because of toilet training by parents. Child is taught where to pass urine and where to go for defecation etc. In this training of bladder and bowel control, child may develop autonomy, or shame and doubt. The task of anal is to develop autonomy. If the parents are supportive without being overprotective and if the child is allowed to function with some independence, he gains some confidence in his autonomy probably by the age of three and prefers love over hate, cooperation over wilfulness, and self-expression over suppression. Autonomy, thus, overbalances shame and doubt and leads to development of confidence that he can control his functions, and also, to some extent, the people around him. Contrary to this, the child may feel angry, foolish and ashamed if parents criticise his faeces and overcontrol his bowel and bladder functioning during the training for toilet. Observations of *sanskaras* convey acceptance to the child and help the parents to train them in appropriate manner.

The children (with more mistrust and doubt in their share) when adults may need help in accepting failures and imperfection as an inherent part of one's life. By accepting the client as he is, the caseworker can reduce his feeling of self-hatred and perfectionism. Overdemanding adults or those who express temper tantrums when asked to assume responsibility may need to be helped to control their impulsive acts. They should be rewarded when they exhibit controls, and one should reinforce their autonomy and independence when exercised. Autonomy and independence are totally different from impulsive acts as these involve rationality and not emotionality.

Genital (Oedipal) Stage

The task for this period is to develop and strengthen initiative, failing which the child develops a strong feeling of guilt. This period extends from 3rd to 6th years of life, i.e., pre-school period. He is now capable of initiating activity, both intellectual as well as motor on his own. How far this initiative is reinforced depends upon how much physical freedom is given to the child and how far his curiosity is satisfied. If he is led to feel bad about his behaviour or his interests, he may grow with a sense of guilt about his self-initiated activities.

Erikson (1950) opines that the child takes first initiative at home when he/she expresses passionate interest in his/her parent of opposite sex. The parents ultimately disappoint him/her. They should try to help the child to identify with the same sex parent, e.g., the girl should be encouraged to identify with mother and the son with the father. In addition to this initiative, the child also attempts to wrest a place for self in the race of siblings for parents affection. He sees the difference between what he wants and what he is asked to do. This culminates into a clear-cut division between the child's set of expanded desires and the parental set of restrictions. He gradually "turns these values (restrictions, i.e., don'ts) into self-punishment". Slowly and gradually, he extracts more initiative from the conflict and grows happily if his initiative gets proper and adequate reinforcement. The caseworker encourages the clients burdened with guilt feelings to take initiative in family as well as in other situations, and works with his social environment to strengthen his capacity to take initiative.

Latency Stage

This stage covers the period from 6 to 11 years, i.e., school age. The child can reason out rationally and can use the tools that adults use. The sexual interests and curiosity (common in genital period) get suppressed till puberty. If encouraged and given opportunity, he gains confidence in his ability to perform and use adult materials. This leads to feeling of industry in him. When unable to use adult materials, he develops inferiority feelings. Such children may develop problems with peers. They need to be encouraged to interact with classmates and be less dependent upon others. If the child has mastered the task of genital period (initiative in place of guilt) he will be able to master the tasks of latency (industry in place of inferiority) also provided he is encouraged to undertake and helped to execute the responsibilities entrusted to him.

Adolescence Stage

This period, regarded as a period of turmoil, usually starts at 12-13 years and can extend upto 18-19 years. The adolescents, during this transitional process from childhood to maturity, behave something like an adult and sometimes like a child. Parents too show their ambivalence to accept them in their new role of an adult in-the-making. This stage exhibits all the psycho-social characteristics of earlier period and only towards the end, all these get resolved into a new set of role (identity) for the adolescent. In order to develop a personal identity, he becomes fan of some hero, starts following certain ideologies, and tries his luck with opposite sex. Indecision and confusion are not uncommon in this stage. Identification with a wrong person shall create problems for him. The task of this age is to develop identity, i.e., values, strengths, skills, various roles, limitations, etc., failing which his identity gets diffused and he fails to know how to behave in different situations. He needs to be helped to deal with the physiological, emotional pressures alongwith pressures from parents, peers, etc.

Group work is more helpful with problem-adolescents. When showing confusion about their role, they can be helped to emulate the group leader or identify with group worker. Parents can handle adolescents properly if educated adequately about the needs and problems of this age.

Similarly, tasks for young adulthood, adulthood and old age are intimacy vs. isolation, generativity vs. stagnation, and ego-integrity vs. despair. These psycho-analytical concepts are helpful in understanding behaviour of the individuals. Apart from these, there are some other tasks described by some other scholars for each stage which according to them are to be achieved for a normal human development.

System Approach

A system is "a complex of elements or components directly or indirectly related to a causal network in such a way that each component is related to atleast some others in a more or less stable way within a particular period of time" (Buckley, 1967). Individuals, families, groups, communities and organisations are regarded as system with certain common properties. Every system is composed of interacting units, each with its own parts and each being part of some larger whole, i.e., each system is a structural part of some other larger system. Each system has its own equilibrium and progression. Changes in one part of a system will bring changes in other parts, thus in the function of whole. Social system is composed of persons or group of persons who interact and influence the behaviour of each unit beyond its component parts, e.g., family which is distinct from its individual members. Sub-system (i.e., units) of this social system are at least partially interrelated within the existing social order. Every system is an entity which is simultaneously both a part and a whole; e.g., family as a whole is a system and an independent unit, and at the same time, it is part of the community which too is a system and an independent unit. Similarly, individuals and family are independent systems and at the same time individuals are part (sub-system) of a bigger system, i.e., family. Every system tries to maintain its homeostasis, i.e., balance which may vary within certain limits without creating stress in the system. Every system, as said earlier, is the part of bigger system, and every system has sub-systems. Caseworkers use this concept to understand individual client and his behaviour by analysing not only him but also his situations which include his family, neighbourhood, etc. Disturbance in one unit or holon (sub-system) will disturb the system of which this unit is a sub-system. For example, when the child is sick, the whole family is disturbed; when there is fight in one family, the whole village feels upset and concerned, etc.

Gestalt

This school of psychology says that the whole is more than the sum of its parts and sees the person as a whole, i.e., not as a biological or as psychological or social being but as a person with all his bio-psycho-social character. Here, it is very near to system approach. System is considered to be more than and different from the sum of its component units. Using this perspective of holism, Hollis (1972) pleads to focus on the gestalt, i.e., "person-in-situation" to understand and help the individual clients better. The reason behind this view is that the person in his situation interacts in a particular way and all this taken together makes one whole. To understand the person, his situation and the interactions, separated from each other, will be gaining half of the truth. Similarly, family cannot be understood in terms of its individual members; rather it should be seen as one whole. According to this theory, (1) normal personality is characterised by unity, integration, consistency and coherence; (2) analysis of the person begins with the whole and proceeds by a differentiation of that whole into its different aspects; and (3) the individual is motivated by self-actualisation. Gestalt therapy advocated by Perls (1958) initiates the worker to concentrate on "here and now" aspects of the interview and explore client's point of view or situation as it is experienced. Gestalt therapists emphasise on awareness of various undesirable elements in his (client) thinking and behaviour so that he can correct his unproductive behaviour and use his potentials for self-actualisation. These approaches are very much used in social casework also.

Behaviourism

This school's thinking is based on the principles of learning, i.e., conditioning, and modelling. According to this theory, every behaviour is a learned one; therefore, all behaviours, including problem-behaviours, can be unlearned. Social workers find operant model more useful in helping their clients. All behaviours---verbal, cognitive and physical—have operant components. The basic characteristic of an operant behaviour is that its rate (of occurrence) is changed by the consequences that follow the behaviour. This is based on the Thorndikes law of effect which says that responses (behaviours) which are followed by satisfying events are more likely to recur.

Likewise, responses that are followed by unsatisfying events (consequences) are less likely to recur. For example, if a child is praised when he steals a pencil of his classmate, he will again steal his and others pencils etc. If he is rebuked or beaten immediately after he shows the stolen pencil, he is likely to stop the stealing. Skinner (1938) restates this principle that "kinds of consequences which follow a behaviour determine the probability of that behaviour occurring in the future. Consequences of the behaviour (responses) have reinforcing properties which either increase or decrease the future occurrence of the response (behaviour). Those consequences (reinforcers), which increase the probability of the behaviour later, are called positive reinforcers. Primary positive reinforcers are food, water and sexual activities. Social workers do not use these reinforcers for obvious reasons. Secondary positive reinforcers acquire reinforcing properties through repeated association with stimuli that have positive reinforcing properties. For example, a teacher says the word 'good' to a child for solving a question and gives him a toffee, the toffee gets paired with 'good'.

Once this pairing is repeated several times, the child will solve the question for the expression 'good' only because for him 'good' becomes as satisfying as the toffee. Smiling, nodding our heads and using positive verbal statements are positive secondary reinforcers used in interviewing by the social caseworkers. A stimulus that follows a behaviour and helps the individual to secure other reinforcers is called generalised reinforcer. A child who gets money or coupon, after solving a mathematical problems, can use this money/coupon to secure other reinforcers like toffees or pens (generalised reinforcer).

To decrease behaviour (responses) negative reinforcement (aversive stimulus) is applied. This happens in casework sessions when we deliberately change the topic of discussion, point out deficiencies in the clients' behaviours, show serious look or refuse to extend the duration of interview etc.

Our certain behaviours which have become problem or inappropriate are those which have been reinforced by the people around us. In helping to work out such problem-behaviours, caseworkers should try to locate the specific reinforcers and tackle them to free the person from his problem-behaviours. This may involve working with family, friends, or the community at large. Similarly, all desirable behaviours of the client should be positively reinforced by the worker and the people who matter to the client.

Socio-anthropological Concepts

We can now try to understand the social aspects of human living. We have discussed that human behaviour as the net product of interaction of biological, psychological and social forces. In the followings paragraphs we will see how various socio-anthropological theories and constructs are useful to understand human behaviour.

Sociological Theories of Human Behaviour

Functionalism, a school in sociology, considers society as a system with parts (institutions etc.) interconnected and interrelated to each other. It is this system, which shapes the human behaviour through socialisation, i.e., learning the culture of society. Culture is "the way of life of its members, the collection of ideas and habits which they learn, share, and transmit from generation to generation" (Linton, 1945). Culture is learned and shared; it determines how society's members think and feel and guides their action and determines their outlook of life and the ways members should behave in their society.

Interactionism, another school in sociology, is concerned with the interaction of individuals, the process of interaction. According to this school, understanding of action requires knowledge of meanings given to their activities by the actors. Meanings are not fixed; rather they are developed, modified and created. The way a situation is defined (perceived) by the actor, has a direct influence over his actions. Interactionism emphasises that actions of the actor are also affected by his interpretation of the way others see him. Every individual develops a self-concept (a picture of what he is) during his interactions with the people around him and this self-concept affects his actions significantly. Thus interactionists understand human behaviour in terms of (the actors') definitions of the situation and self (i.e., self-concepts). Interactionism implies that roles are often vague and unclear; therefore, there is always a room for negotiating and manoeuvring of roles which are considered as fixed by functionalists. Walsh (1972) argues that human behaviour is not determined by the system. In fact, man constructs his own social world. The *labelling theory*, propounded by Howard S. Becker (1974), an interactionist, is quite important for social workers. According to this theory, social groups create deviance by making the rules whose infraction (violation) constitutes deviance. When someone is labelled as deviant (thief, criminal, mental patient, etc.), he starts behaving in that role. An act becomes deviant when others perceive and regard it as deviant. Goffman (1968) also opines that institutionalisation of a person (in mental hospital or jail etc.) confirms the label and the individual slowly takes over his new role of a deviant (a prisoner or a mental patient). Social workers should avoid labelling and see that parents and neighbours do not label the young ones negatively. All these theories are supplementary and help in explaining behaviour occurring in different situations and conditions.

Organisational Theory

The organisational theory "reflects a significant trend of social change----the increase of large organisations of men, whose members' significance is in their contribution to the organisation's goals, rather than in their personal qualities". Impact of bureaucratic organisations on the clients functioning is crucial in the study and diagnosis of the 'person-in-his situation'.

Social caseworkers have, of late, learnt to note the "emotional impact of bureaucratic existence as a source of the client's emotional malfunctioning and social maladjustment". This theory also calls upon the caseworkers to examine organisations in which they work, the effects of organisational variables upon staff and client relations, the structural features of organisations and the issues and dilemmas pertaining to them.

Values, Norms and Beliefs

Values comprise of ideas which are preferred, described in other words, what is good, right, wise or beneficial. Values are generally expressed in terms of 'shoulds'. Values are implanted early in a person's life and once they are fixed, serve as a guide in choosing behaviour and in forming attitudes. They become part of superego. Values change through day-to-day behaviour, regulated by norms. Values are developed and reinforced and do not develop spontaneously. Values are re-learned, e.g., in group work sessions members re-learn the desirable values, viz., riches of others should be treated as mud, other's wife should be seen as mother, and the like. Social work has its own values which are embedded in democratic values.

Norms mean any rule or standard that defines appropriate and acceptable behaviour, what people should or should not do, think or feel in any given situation. Norms seen as expression of values are standards of behaviour shared by a larger segment of society. Norms are formally expressed through law. Informal norms are expressed through social customs or folkways and mores. Breaking of folkways may not be seriously taken by the society but defying the mores invariably invokes social sanction against the violators. Norms can be studied by observing the behaviour of a certain group of individuals in a society and knowing how others respond to that behaviour. A person who violates norms beyond a certain limit is labelled as 'abnormal'.

Beliefs are ideas about the nature of social world, supernatural reality, a person or an object which one believes to be true and acts accordingly. Beliefs may be based on facts or may be without factual evidence. According to Ellis (1973), beliefs generate emotions. To cite an example, when Mr. B. abuses Mr. A, he (Mr. A) gets angry or sad with Mr. B. because he believes that this abuse has lowered his prestige, status, etc. Sadness/anger is the result of the belief about being abused and not of the event (abusing). Individual beliefs play very important role in the behaviour of a person, therefore, caseworker should try to tackle and manage these beliefs.

The therapeutic concepts related to beliefs have been very well developed by Albert Ellis. His approach (practice theory) is named as Rational Emotive Therapy.

According to Ellis (1973), practically, all "emotional disturbances stem from demanding or whining instead of from wanting or desiring". People who feel anxious, depressed or hostile do not merely wish to prefer something but also command, dictate, insist that they achieve this thing. Typically, they demand that they be outstandingly achieving and/or greatly approved by others, and they thereby make themselves disturbed when they fail to achieve these demands. Or, they insist that others treat them considerately or fairly, and they create feelings of severe anger or hostility when others do not. Or, they dictate that life and the world be easy, enjoyable and unfrustrating, and they manufacture over rebelliousness, self-pity and inertia when conditions are difficult.

Just about every time one feels disturbed or upset, instead of merely displeased, frustrated or disappointed, one is stoutly convincing one self that something is awful rather than inconvenient or disadvantageous. One frequently believes (1) "It is awful that I am imperfect and am disapproved"; (2) "It is terrible that you are treating me less than ideally"; (3) "Or, it is horrible that the world is so onerous and ungratifying."

When one awfulises or catastrophises about reality, he is setting up an unverifiable, magical, unempirical hypothesis. For, to hold that anything is awful, terrible, or horrible, rather than unfortunate, unpleasant, or painful, is to hold (1) it is all bad and can have no good in it; (2) it is more than bad or disadvantageous; (3) because it is unpleasant, it should not and muse not exist; (4) one cannot stand its existence; (5) one has to be utterly miserable about it; and (6) one is a worthless person if he cannot immediately change himself, others, and the universe so that this awful thing no longer exists. All these hypotheses are definitional and cannot be proved or disproved. They essentially represent demons which one invents and is governed by. And, once one devoutly believes in them, these will create anxiety, guilt feelings of worthlessness, depression, and hostility.

The simple and effective solution to the problem of human disturbance, obviously, is to exercise the demons, i.e., the unrealistic beliefs. Give up the demandingness and whining and presenting. Underline the 'awfulness' and 'terribleness' of noxious stimuli and fully acknowledge that nothing in the whole universe is more than very inconvenient and disadvantageous, and that there is no reason why pains and displeasures should not, must not exist.

Humans in other words, can eliminate their feelings of horror, hopelessness and hostility (and retain their appropriate feelings of disappointment and annoyance) if they will truly join the human race, give up all pretentions of being superhuman, of encouraging gods or devils, or of living in a perfectly easy, immediately gratifying world. If they practise living rigorously in empirical reality, strongly desiring and actively working to improve that reality but not grandiosely dictating that it be otherwise than it indoubtably is, they can reach a point where they rarely upset themselves and therefore rarely have to counteract their awfulising.

Emotional disorder according to Ellis tends to stem from some form of two simple words: "Its awful", or "How horrible", or "It's terrible". If one rigidly holds these ideas about anything, he will be basically upsettable and often disturbed. If one wants to eliminate one's disturbance, he can substitute two other simple words: "Tough luck", "Too bad", or "How unfortunate". As long as one really thinks through and believes and not merely parrots the confirmable meaning behind these words (namely, that it is too bad that the people and the world are imperfect but that it is tough, that's the way it is and that's the way it may even continue to be), he will tend to be undisturable and often more interested in working to change obnoxious reality.

Role and Status

Every individual occupies certain position or status like that of a mother, professor, director, etc., within system (family, institute, etc.). Every status stands related to some other statuses and demonstrates its interconnection with these ones. Statuses like mother and child, teacher and student, neighbour, etc., imply a relationship to one another. Ascribed status is usually fixed at birth and is determined by inheritance or biological factors. Opposed to this is the achieved status which is the result of purposive action and choice of the individual. It (status) spells out a set of rights and obligations that regulate the transactions with individuals of other statuses. Role concept is used to denote behaviours prescribed for an individual occupying a designated status. It refers to how the holder of a status should act towards an individual with whom he is obliged to interact because of his particular status. Anthropologists define role as "culturally determined patterns of behaviour" and "culturally defined social norms which dictate reciprocal action". Perlman (1962) explains role as "a person's organised patterns of modes of behaviour, fashioned by the status or functions he carries in relation to one or more persons. Such a behaviour pattern is selected, shaped and coloured by several dynamic factors: (1) the person's needs and drives---what he wants consciously and unconsciously; (2) the person's ideas of the mutual obligations and expectations that have been invested (by custom, tradition, convention) in the particular status and functions he undertakes; and (3) the compatibility or conflict between the person's conception of obligations and expectations and those held by the other person(s) with whom he is in reciprocation." In this explanation, both social and individual determinants of role behaviour have been taken into consideration. Role, here, has been conceived as a bridge between psychological and social processes as stated by Ackerman (1954).

The concept of role has become so important that Boehm (1959) defines casework in terms of role performance and uses it for purposes of diagnostic classification. During the study phase, the worker is expected to clarify his own role *vis-à-vis* the role of the client, thus helps the applicant to behave in the role of a client. Role analysis helps in focusing on the person-situation strength as well as deficiencies by studying the role expectation, role reciprocity, role complementarity, role conflict, role ambiguity, etc. *Role expectation* refers to informal codes of propriety, the expected behaviour from the individual according to his status by others in interaction with him. This is enforced by ridicule, prestige, etc. *Role complementarity* exists when the reciprocal role of a role partner is carried automatically without difficulty and in expected ways; for example, mother's bahaviour towards the child. There cannot be a mother without a child and vice versa, therefore, one role is complementary to the other role. Role complementarity is dependent upon *role reciprocation* by the role partners in a particular situation as in the case of mother and child. Each role is complementary to other one only when each role involved is played properly and adequately, i.e., when it is reciprocated as expected. Thus, the mother-child, teacher-student roles are reciprocal and complementary. Failure in role complementarity, according to Spiegel (1971) is (1) because one or both parties are not familiar with the roles which they are expected to assume (cognitive discrepancy), (2) when ego or alter (teacher or student) requires roles that the other does not posses (discrepancy of roles), (3) when roles are not accepted by at least one of the role partners (allocative discrepancy), (4) because of lack of required resources (instrumental means) like money, knowledge, skill etc., and (5) because of a discrepancy in cultural value orientations which is seen in inter-continental or inter-community or inter-caste marriages. Roles 'ascribed' are automatically (mother, brother etc.) received because of age, sex, occupation, etc. These may be 'achieved' by virtue of the job one has taken or they may be 'adopted' by the individual to satisfy his some personal needs. Roles are 'assumed' also in playful mood (casually).

Role conflict involves a situation "in which the incumbent of a local position perceives that he is confronted with incompatible expectations". Role conflict may occur for example when the role of school social worker is interpreted as maintaining order by the principal whereas co-social workers interpret his role as enhancing the social functioning of the students. *Role incongruency* (defined as a situation in which one's perception of his own role is different from the expectations of significant others) can also cause role conflict. *Role ambiguity* includes those roles which are given no place in the social system and that "it lacks regularised expectation for what and how its occupants are to operate". According to Perlman (1962), the aged, foster parents suffer from the role ambiguity.

Ecological Constructs

Very often it is alleged that the social caseworkers become more involved with the individual to the total neglect of his environment. This does not seem to be justified, when social work because of its 'social' accent as differentiated from 'psychological' has been known to be concerned with understanding of the individual in his social and physical environment in his efforts to help people to improve their social functioning. The ecological concepts provide a safer approach in which the risk of viewing and dealing with the individual as separate from his situation gets reduced to the minimum. This helps us to integrate individualised services for individuals, groups, etc., with social action to improve environment. This model/approach emphasises on functions "to promote natural growth and development of people and to influence the environment to be supportive of such growth and development". Efforts are directed to the patterns and potentials of the client and qualities of the environment or both "in order to improve the transactions between them".

Important concepts are related to (a) the transactions between the people and their environment, (b) attributes achieved by individuals in their interaction with environment, and (c) the environmental qualities (Germain and Gitterman, 1970) as discussed below:

Transactional Concepts

Ecology, as a science, studies the relationship between living organisms and their total environment and how they achieve and maintain (or fail) adoptive balance (or a goodness of fit). Ecological sciences help in maintaining a safe environment and improving its quality for better biological, psychological, cognitive and social growth and environment of the living organisms, specially the human beings. Adaptive balance is always attempted to be achieved by all the living organisms. This adaptive process in the case of the human beings is social, psychological and cultural apart from being biological. This adaptive capacity of the human being, because of his large brain and diverse gene pool for recombination, enables him, through language, symbolisation, knowledge and belief systems, to adapt to the ever changing physical and social environment. Today's adaptive demands, specially in highly urbanised and industrial towns, pose serious problems for the individuals. It crosses, many a time, his biological, psychological and social capacity to adapt to these changes engineered by the man himself. In this process, man may have to depend upon social and cultural processes to achieve the adaptive balance by effecting needed changes in the environment and in himself. Like physical environment, social environment can also be polluted by factors like ill-designed housing projects, haphazard growth of industries, poverty, racism, sexism etc. These create adaptive imbalance resulting in disorganised behaviour, interpersonal stress and physical disorders etc. Such pollutions, though is the result of man's efforts to achieve a goodness of fit (adaptive balance) with their environment, make adaptation of the man more difficult. In ecological terms, "upsets in the usual or desired fit can be conceptualised as stress". Presence or absence of internal/external stimuli may precipitate/cause stress. Stress becomes unmanageable once the normally available coping strategies fail to achieve the desired purpose or when the demands are perceived by the individual as one beyond his capabilities.

Personality variables, like motivation, self-esteem, problem-solving skills, decision-making capacity and acting according to the decisions, help in coping because of their reciprocal relationship with the environment. Motivation is dependent upon the incentives and rewards given by the environment. (Thus, it is in relationship with the environment). Similarly, self-esteem and control of anxiety are dependent upon social support available from the environment. Problem-solving skills depend upon the training given by the family, school and other similar institutions in the social environment. Transactional concepts can be summarised as under:

1. The man must get suitable environmental (social as well as physical) nutriments at the desirable moments of life to release his genetic potentials and accelerate his growth and development in biological, cognitive, sensory-perceptual, emotional and social areas. This view is supported by the biological theory that human functioning and development are the result of a complex interaction between polygenetic potentials and environmental releasers, stimuli or nutriments (Dobzhansky, 1976). Theories of adult socialisation and competence suggest that man's personality development does not stop at any point of life, it rather continues to develop and even to change over the years because of

various life-events and processes. Man achieves freedom (in various degrees) from biological and environmental limits by virtue of his culture and freedom from his own past histories, by his own genetic potential for growth and development and the acquisition of adaptive abilities through learning.

2. Biological and personality theorists define adaptation as an active, creative process by which man changes his environment to meet his needs and aspirations, and by which he actively changes himself to conform to acceptable or unchangeable environmental requirements.
3. Adaptation is achieved by migration to a new environment also.

Human Attributes

Sense of identity, competence, autonomy and human relatedness are the attributes which are achieved in the process of growth and development through interaction with environment.

Identity, discussed by Erikson (1950) also, develops from the interaction with other human beings. It starts with the first relationship with mother and moves of family, neighbourhood, school etc. According to life model, its development continues throughout the life. Events of life alongwith others opinion about self in the process of living, continue to shape and reshape the sense of identity, self-image and self-esteem. It does not stop at adolescence. *Competence* comprises of "the sum of the person's successful experiences in the environment". Competence is measured in terms of the effects of the person on his environment. This is again a lifelong issue. *Autonomy*, a capacity for self-regulation, refers to inner and outer freedom. An autonomous person relatively acts freely and is relatively free from his internal demands because of his relationship and interaction with other human beings and nature. Autonomy means freedom from subjugation to the internal demands as well as environmental demands. Sense of identity, competence and feeling of relatedness all contribute to the achievement of authority which continues throughout the total life-span. *Human relatedness* is considered to be biological and social imperative for the human being. Relationship is always nourishing and an essential need for the proper growth and development of child and this continues for the whole life, more so in the old age.

Environmental Qualities

The environment has two layers----social environment and physical environment; the textures of environment are time and space. Ecologists exhibit more interest in social networks and bureaucratic organisations----the two main components of social environment. Social environment and physical environment interact in a very complex way, each influencing and shaping the other. Values, beliefs, knowledge, economy, etc., influence the way people react to the physical environment and in turn physical environment including climate shapes our pattern of relating with others and social structures etc. Culture and interaction between physical and social environments affect human behaviour, and human behaviour in turn also affects or changes the physical and social environment including cultural norms, values, beliefs, etc.

Social networks represent "a system of relationship in which the linkages between and among the members are considered influential in behaviour". Network includes friends, neighbours, workmates or self-help groups. Social networks serve our affective and instrumental needs. Effectively, they lend us support, enhance our self-esteem etc., and instrumentally they provide us resources, informations, knowledge and skills to deal with our problems.

Time and *space* are another important concepts in this approach. The meaning of time to everyone varies. Value of past, present and future varies from individual to individual. We use time to be involved with others or to maintain distance from others. Similarly, space is important, e.g., setting of the room influences our interaction with the people in room. Locked cells of mental hospitals and well-furnished rooms of the company executives affect us differently.

These concepts, if used, give us a better understanding of the problem, person, and place and the social emphasis in social casework gets fully vindicated in it.

Human Needs

In social work, efforts are made to meet the needs of the client system (individual, group or community). *Need* is defined as one which is necessary for either a person or a social system to function within reasonable expectations. Need is not synonymous with want. Non-fulfilment of need inhibits the functioning of the individual and retards his development. Problem can also be defined in terms of needs. Problem is a need not being met adequately and appropriately. Social workers attend to these problems/needs. When the society's mechanism fails to meet the needs of the system (individual, group, organisation), resulting in an imbalance between the system and the world around him (i.e., personal-social imbalance), it leads to a stressful situation. A *stressful situation* is one which is "beyond the conscious control of the person involved in them". Stress affects our social functioning adversely.

Needs may be physical, psychological and social. Charlotte Towle (1945) has described needs related to physical welfare (food, shelter etc.), emotional and intellectual growth, relationship with the people around, and to spiritual satisfaction. These needs affect human development and vary according to age and life situation of the person. Needs of a child, and of an adolescent, are different from the needs of an old man. Abraham Maslow (1954) has described needs in the following hierarchical manner:

1. Physiological needs---food, water, air, etc.
2. Safety needs—avoidance of pain and damage to body.
3. Needs for belongingness and love---sense of security, being loved etc.
4. Esteem needs—status and acceptance in one's social groups.
5. Needs for self-actualisation---expression of potentialities and capabilities.
6. Needs for cognitive understanding---understanding of self and the world.

The first two needs (related to physical needs) are to be satisfied before one longs for satisfaction of belongingness. Physical needs can be termed as primary needs because these are basic to one's survival. Only after physical needs are met, one puts efforts to meet his secondary needs, like status and fame in the society, though many physical needs (specially in the early childhood and advanced old age) cannot be met without relationship with the others around. Economists also categorise needs (necessities) basically into three: (1) necessary, (2) comfortable, and (3) luxurious. Necessary needs are the bare minimum required for one's survival, whereas comfortable are helpful to increase the efficiency of the person and increase his satisfaction in living, and the luxurious are wastage of one's resources and affect his efficiency adversely.

Social workers should see if the needs of the client have been met adequately and how these are affecting his social functioning; whether these needs, if not satisfied earlier, can be met now, how its meeting will affect the family and other system and how it will accelerate the development of the client; if the client's approach to fulfil his needs is appropriate in the situation, and cultural factors are affecting his style and efforts to meet his needs etc.

Vedantic Concepts

One set of concepts used in the Vedanta is Brahma, Vishnu and Mahesh. Lord Brahma is the one who has created this universe; Lord Vishnu protects it, and Lord Mahesh will destroy it. Out of these three potentialities, Vishnu is the greatest because he is the protector of the universe. These gods (cosmic forces) are, in fact, (I presume), three different dimensions of our personality, i.e., creative, protective and destructive. At one point in Vedanta, man is said to be the creator of the world (मन एव विरिञ्चत्वम्: योगवशिष्ठ, 3/3/84). These and many other writings lead us to believe that these three gods represent nothing but the three different potentialities of our personality which need to be assessed and strengthened. The controversy may arise about the role of Mahesh because of various roles ascribed to him. However, it needs to be understood that basically it is he who controls destructive forces and its agents (Upadhyay, 1993).

Sattvic, Rajasic and Tamasic

Personality's another three dimensions have been expressed by the concepts of *Satva*, *Rajas* and *Tamas*. Satva is pure, free from desires and selfish actions. It is more akin to submissive nature, selfless, socially oriented, super-normal and saintly qualities of the man. Compared to this is Rajas which is assertive, active, dominant and one which seeks to acquire, possess and enjoy sense objects. Tamas is aggressive, impulsive, selfish and greedy and seeks self-satisfaction at the cost of the society. (Vegetarian foods like fruits, vegetables build up a Sattvic temperament; rich foods like milk, dry fruits, etc., help to build Rajasic temperament; and foods like meet, wine, etc., give rise to a Tamasic temperament, according to our scriptures). Personality can be understood, and explained in these terms also and efforts may be undertaken in casework to strengthen the productive, protective and assertive parts of personality to live a meaningful life.

Gyan (Knowledge)

Once one gets knowledge of any object or situation in full, his perception of reality is complete. Knowledge as per Vedanta is real only when it helps us to see and experience the reality. This knowledge then leads one to most appropriate action and frees him from 'askti' (bondage, i.e., emotional indulgence). Once, one is free from bondage, he can perform his duties without bothering about the results. In such situations, the only motive to act should be one's duty, i.e., to act according to one's role (कर्मण्येवाधिकारस्ते—*Gita*, 2/47). Any and every action with desirable motive is a good action. One has to enjoy acting and doing his duty. If one works for certain fruits, he may work inefficiently and take short-cut methods and is sure to suffer from anxiety when he fails to achieve his goal. Therefore, action should be guided by the sense of duty and not by the expectations of results. To evaluate this doctrine's applicability, one should ponder over and practise it before he can be convinced of its practicability and utility. Role is one's duty (धर्म) and overtaking of other's role is prohibited (*Gita*, 3/35).

According to *Yogvashistha*, mind has potentialities to create anything and everything. Mind gets what it wants to get. It is capable of creating anything it wants. It has unlimited power to achieve anything and everything. Things appear in the way we want them to appear, thus untrue may appear true. Exercise (repeating the desired behaviour—अभ्यास) is the key to success. Pleasure and displeasure depend upon our mind. Mental problems (*ādhi*) give birth to physical problems (*vyādhi*), i.e., the psychosomatic concept of diseases as given by Yogvashistha.

Anekāntvād (अनेकान्तवाद), according to Jainism, a cult of Hinduism, means that everything has more than one characteristic aspect, quality or factor. We, most of the time, see only one aspect of a thing and consider this aspect as the total aspect of that object to which Anekāntvād is opposed. It pleads for looking at everything from different angles to understand it in totality as everything has different aspects. This principle believes that there is a perpetual change in the object of our attention----be it metals, creature or any such thing. It further assumes that everything consists of mutually contradictory qualities or characteristics also. We see or perceive a thing from a particular angle or perspective and this particular angle or perspective determines our perception of the things. In other words, our perception is coloured by the colour of our goggles when the real colour of the thing (i.e., the reality) is different from the colour of our goggles (perspective) used by us at different times. More or less, the same thing has been said by our saint-poet Tulsidas in *Ram Charitmanas* (जाकी रही भावना जैसी, हरि मूरति देखी तिन तैसी).

Syātvād (स्यात्वाद) is another principle of Jainism which supplements the principle of Anekāntāvād. For example, when one says that this animal looks like a horse, he says two things at a time, i.e., this may be a horse and may not be a horse. Thus, Syātvād is a way to express different aspects of a thing, though this expresses only one aspect of a thing at a time prominently and keeps the other aspect of the object in background. When one says that this is black, he emphasises black aspect of the thing. At the same time, its other aspects are kept in background. Syātvād and the detailed description of these methods of expression are mentioned in 'Saptahengi' of Jainism. Expression prescribed by Saptahengi, for example, are: (1) perhaps this is an earthen pot, (2) perhaps this is not an earthen pot, etc.

Anekāntvād directs the therapist to look for other aspects of the situation and accept the present picture with a question mark. This calls for looking for other alternative aspects of the situation to understand the situation more realistically and in totality. Thus, these concepts can be profitably utilised in social casework practice.

Functional and Diagnostic Schools in Social Casework

Functional social casework was developed by Jessie Taft (1937) and Virginia Robinson (1942), the then faculty members of Pennsylvania School of Social Work. Taft and Robinson, both were influenced in their work, by the philosophy and teachings of Herbert Mead and John Dowey and later by Otto Rank, a disciple of Freud, who broke away from him in the later part of his life. The functional school was further developed and sustained by Kenneth Pray (1949) and Ruth Smalley (1967). Its development can be regarded as a reaction to the diagnostic school of social work which was heavily influenced by the Freudian concepts of personality and treatment in the 1920s and for many years thereafter.

Diagnostic school, based on scientific (psychic) determinism, believed that the client is the product of his past, that he is ill and needs treatment. The client is diagnosed and subjected to treatment. The presenting problem is regarded as merely an expression of deeper psycho-pathological condition. The therapist (caseworker) assumes sole responsibility for treating the client. In this approach, the client is helped to readjust to his past events which are affecting his current functioning. This view of psycho-analysis and its effect on casework practice continued till 1950s when neo-Freudians changed the concept of man from 'the created' to the creator self.

Functionalists considered human activity as purposive and deliberate and not only as the result of pushes by internal and external forces. Human personality is considered as always in the "process of becoming", constantly working towards realisation of all its capacities. A human being is regarded as fashioner of his own fate, and capable of creating and using inner and outer experiences to shape his own ends. In contrast to diagnostic, functionalism emphasises present experience and its power to release growth potential. Treatment used in diagnostic was replaced by the concept of service and helping process in which the relationship (a dynamic interaction between the helper and client) is given pivotal position. When diagnostic school holds the caseworker responsible for setting and carrying out treatment goals, the functionalists view clients as capable of using the present situation, the helping relationship, actualising innate capacities, and resolving problems. As opposed to diagnostic, functionalist helps the clients only in one phase or fragment (part) of the total problem because of the assumption that change in anyone hurting area of his life could bring in a 'salutary effect' on the total psychological equilibrium of the client. Human problems are caused by destructive use of relationship, therefore, the interaction between the helper and client is used for positive change through the experience, gained in the casework relationship, of a positive, productive and constructive way of utilising the self in the helping process.

"Time symbolises the whole problems of living in that it represents simultaneously both the need to accept limitation and the difficulty in doing so." Emphasis is upon the present moments and present relationships. In contrast to data collection (study) for diagnosis, important to treatment in diagnostic school, the functional school considers diagnosis as "a developing process, worked out by the client himself, as he uses the agency service, and as he tests his own capacities, and needs..." Functionalists reject the stance of diagnostic school of helping from a pedestal of superiority assumed by the worker.

Functionalists give utmost importance to the use of agency function in helping process. This is considered as unifying and direction-giving to the helping process. It gives focus and contents to the helping interaction. It is because of the use of the agency function that social work is called an 'institutionalised profession'. Unlike diagnosticians, functionalists believe that agency provides "reality boundaries within which the ex-client can test and discover his ability to work out his problem and make a satisfying adjustment or readjustment to the wider realities". "The worker sets up the conditions as found in his agency function and procedure; the client... tries to accept, to reject, to attempt to control, or to modify that function until he finally comes to terms with it enough to define or discover what he wants, if anything, from this situation" (Taft, 1937). Man, according to functionalist, has an innate striving (push) towards growth of an integrated self. The juncture at which a client approaches the helper is the time of growth and as such it provides basic conditions and ingredients necessary for mobilisation towards self-help. The first separation a child weathers is birth, i.e., separation from mother's body. If child's relations, particularly with mother, have been positive and constructive, the 'will' has learned to accept the inevitability of separation and to accept reality limitations as its own. The helping relationship is the growth-releasing situation in which the client has full freedom of choice and self-determination. Functionalists help the client to face, understand, accept and deal constructively with the chosen realities of his own situation, i.e., his self-capacities and the facts of his social situation.

The usual model of casework in practice is an eclectic model which has been enriched by both the functional and diagnostic schools of thinking.

After discussing the concepts from sociology, anthropology, ecology, Vedant and functional/diagnostic schools etc. the focus will, now, be on relationship, an extremely important concept in social casework practice. It deserves to be discussed separately, therefore the chapter that follows is on relationship.

4

Relationship

Value of relationship can be gauged from the fact that no help can be administered to a client of casework services without positive relationship. In fact, society is society because of relationship. Society is said to be the totality in which human beings engage in social relations, or, in other words, it is a "network of relationships". Every human action contains an element of relationship. This relationship in turn affects one's thinking, feelings and action. When we think of something sitting all alone in our room, it is in terms of our relationship with people, may be friends, family members, relatives, co-workers, or public in general. Our very existence is in terms of our relationship with people around us. Lives cannot be lived without relationship to other people. All institutions are built around relationship. Institutions minus relationship have no existence. Help or troubles emanate from our relationship with the fellow human beings. Whether one is troubled or helped by someone, relationship does exist between them.

Thus, relationship is an 'emotional bond' between people who interact with each other. Our interaction is initially determined by the bond we have with the person concerned and in turn this interaction either strengthens or weakens this bond. It may, in other words, make us friendly or hostile to each other. It can be said to be a 'transmission belt' of communication, a set of attitudes and responses between the interacting units. According to Northen (1969), relationship consists "primarily of emotional responses which ebb and flow from person to person as human behaviour evokes different affective reactions". According to Perlman (1957), it is a condition in which two persons with some common interest between them, long-term or temporary, interact with feelings. Relationship leaps from one person to the other at the moment when some kind of emotion moves between them. They may both express or invest the same kind of emotion; they may express or invest different or even opposing emotions or ...one may express or invest emotion and the other will receive it and be responsive to it. In any case, a charge or current of feeling must be experienced between two persons. Whether this interaction creates a sense of union or of antagonism, the two persons are for the time being 'connected' or 'related' to each other. "The essence of the relationship has been called an interplay, a mutual emotional exchange, an attitude, a dynamic interaction, a medium, a connection between two persons, a professional meeting, and a mutual process." The purpose of the professional relationship is described as creating an atmosphere, the development of personality, a better solution of the client's problem, the means for carrying out function, stating and focusing reality and emotional problems, and helping the client make a more acceptable adjustment to a personal problem (Biestek, 1957).

Coyle (1948) considers relationship as "a discernible process by which people are connected to each other and around which the group takes its shape and form" while Biestek (1957) considers it as "the dynamic interactions of attitudes and emotions". Thus, relationship is a natural phenomenon occurring between persons interacting with each other singly or in groups. Relationship can be, then, shaped, manipulated or developed as we intend it to be.

Relationship in Social Work

How relationship can and should be used to help persons with problem has been a serious concern of not only social work but of other professions too like that of psychiatry, psychology etc. Social work always recognised the importance of human interaction and attempted to use relationship in a conscious and deliberate manner to benefit the people it worked with. Social work literature is full of description of relationship from various angles only because of its great importance in a helping process. Richmond (1917), in her earliest work, has pleaded for an intensive study and use of social relationship in social casework. Social caseworker's focus should be on "skill in discovering the social relationships by which a given personality has been defined; an ability to get at the central core of the difficulty in these relationships; and power to utilise the direct action of mind upon mind in their adjustment".

None can deny the utility and importance of human relationship in promoting change and development. When relationship is established and used by a social worker consciously, purposefully and deliberately to help client(s), it is called a *professional relationship*. It is characterised by "conscious purposiveness growing out of the knowledge of what must go into achieving its goal" (Perlman, 1957). In fact, relationship is the channel of entire casework process. It is the medium through which knowledge of human nature and social interaction are used, and through which, they are given the opportunity to make choices, both about receiving and using the help. Thus, one finds that "relationship is the basis of all help".

Characteristics of Relationship

As discussed earlier, professional relationship is formed with a particular purpose and it terminates once that purpose is served. This is in addition to the normative purpose of all professional relationships, i.e., some kind of change in, or development of, human beings leading to a "personally satisfying and socially useful life". It is the individualised purpose which is unique to every relationship and is set to be achieved in each case. This purpose sets and determines how persons in the professional relationship will behave towards one another.

The conscious, purposive and deliberate efforts to develop a helping relationship contains elements of

(1) purpose and concern for the client system;
(2) expectations;
(3) empathy and clear communication;
(4) genuineness and acceptance; and
(5) authority.

Purpose and Concern

The purpose and concern for the client involves the worker's care for everything that happens to the client in such a way that the client feels and realises the worker's concern for him. According to Fromm (1956), it consists of "sense of responsibility, care, respect, knowledge of other human beings and the wish to further their lives". It means that we involve ourselves deeply in the affairs of client without getting obsessed by it. Keith-Lucas (1972) observes that concern implies serving the interest of the client. Concern for other includes meanings expressed in concepts like understanding, warmth, unconditional respect, and liking etc., which is communicated through punctuality, taking consent before making home/ school visits, observing cultural norms for showing respects, attentive listening, questioning and commenting as and when desirable for helping the client. Our knowledge, skills and experience are to be used to foster movement in the client towards the desired and consciously determined purpose. It is this purpose that improves the social functioning within the orbit of social work profession and guides the relationship with the client. The purpose of establishing relationship is known to and accepted by both worker and client. Relationship is established around this purpose.

Expectations

Persons frequently tend to anticipate what gains, losses or experiences will accrue to them out of a particular event or contact with a person. We all experience how expectations of the future affect our behaviour in the present, and which, in turn, influences our future behaviour and our sense of security and well-being. Expectations are major determinants of behaviour. How client's expectancies are confirmed or disconfirmed will affect his relationship with the worker and their interaction within it. This warrants clarification about the expectations in precise terms each has from the other.

In general, three types of expectations are always found in the client-worker relationship. *One* is, how the worker feels about the client's ability and desire to change, and his own ability to effect change in the client's situation. To be effective, the worker must be convinced of the "power of the push" towards self-development, i.e., the client can change given appropriate help and support. The *second* is, what are the expectations of the client from the worker? Client cannot be effectively helped unless his expectations are met by the workers' behaviour. In other words, the expectations of the worker and that of the client should be in accord as to what will be going on between them in the transactions between them. The more discrepancy between what the client expects, and what happens in the client-worker transactions, the lesser are the chances for the client to continue in the relationship. The *third* expectation is of positive results following the interaction with the worker. This involves faith of the client in the efficacy of the treatment process and the worker's professional competence and helpfulness. The worker must confirm or work out these expectations to seek deeper involvement and continuance of the client in the helping process.

Empathy

Perlman (1979) explains this as "feeling with and into another person, being able to get into his shoes". Thus, one tries to know what the client feels and experiences without getting lost in the process. Rogers (1966) explains empathy as "the perceiving of the internal frame of reference of another with accuracy, and with the emotional components which pertain thereto, as if one were the other person but without ever losing the 'as if' condition". Empathy communicates that the worker understands the depth of the feeling of the client and that he is with him. It requires an imaginative capacity. Comments like the following communicate empathy: "I understand that you are upset". "I can understand how perturbed you are because of...", "It must be difficult for you to..." Empathy does not mean the loss of objectivity. It can be learned and developed so that the therapist can understand the world of the client "as he sees it".

The helper can be effective in communicating empathic understanding when he

(1) concentrates with intensity upon the helpee's expressions, both verbal and non-verbal;
(2) concentrates on responses that are interchangeable with the helper;
(3) formulates his responses in language that is most attuned to the helpee;
(4) responds in a feeling tone similar to that communicated by the helpee;
(5) is most responsive (interacts with the helpee);
(6) having established an interchangeable base of communication, moves tentatively towards expanding and clarifying the helpee's experiences at higher levels;
(7) concentrates upon what is not being expressed by the helpee (the deepest level of empathy involves filling in what is missing rather than simply dealing with what is present); and
(8) employs the helpee's behaviour as the best guideline to assess the effectiveness of his response.

Communication plays a very vital role in establishing relationship and is most important of all (see chapter on 'Communication').

Genuineness and Acceptance

To be genuine and congruent, the worker relies on his moment to moment felt experiences in his relationship with the client. *Genuineness* should reflect from the worker's behaviour and permeate his all interactions with the client. A genuine and congruent relationship consists of a consistent and honest openness and behaviour matching with the verbalised intentions and values of social work. The worker should be consistent in his communications and behaviour towards the client. If he says that he is honest, he must accept it when he commits mistakes. Similarly, his claim to help the client must get expressed in his efforts. *Congruence* implies workers being what he feels inside. The Indian scriptures emphasise this when they exhort men to be consistent in their thinking, talking and acting upon (मनसा, वाचा, कर्मणा). If we are genuinely interested in the client's welfare, it is bound to show up in our behaviour. It means, then, that we must try to translate our inner feelings into behaviour if it does not show up properly. To be genuine and congruent, one must understand oneself in terms of one's capabilities, attitudes, prejudices, personal values, temperament, etc. Knowledge of agency and its policies, procedures, role, commitment to the client's welfare will facilitate being genuine. Rogers (1954) has emphasised this as one of the most important factors (others being empathy and positive regards) for effecting change in clients.

Acceptance, as usually understood, is to accept (like) the person but not all his actions. This notion of acceptance leaves enough scope for criticism of the client's certain actions though out of goodwill only. Gandhiji has also said the same thing when he asks to "hate the sin and not the sinner". Some authors explain this in terms of receiving what the clients offer of themselves with a respect for their capacity and worth, belief in their capacity to grow and change, and with awareness that their behaviour can be understood as a means to cope with the situations. Acceptance is to express one's goodwill towards the client in spite of his weaknesses or unhealthy behaviour. Acceptance implies that the worker considers the client as a person with feelings, thoughts and experiences unique to him.

It emphasises the worker's faith in the capacity of the clients for self-determination and self-direction. Acceptance assumes that people behave and act as they ought to because of the particular nature of the situation in which they are. They are what they ought to be because of their environment, capacities and other endowments. Acceptance is communicated through expressing concern and respect to the client.

Authority

Social workers have always been concerned with the use of authority as a tool to help clients who need protective kind of services and whose ego functioning is poor. Authority is the power delegated to the practitioners by society (client and agency) because of his status and expertise in the field. *Power* denotes the inherent ability or the admitted right to rule, govern or determine. *Authority* refers to the power because of rank or office to give commands, enforce obedience and make a decision. Herein, the worker (practitioner) occupying a certain position in the agency is perceived as having power to influence the client to move towards the desired goal of change and growth. Authority, thus, gets vested in the worker because of his status in the agency (social or bureaucratic authority) and because of his knowledge and experience (psychological or professional authority). The client considers the worker as competent to help him, direct his activities and guide him in solution of his problems, thus, experience security in his relationship with the worker. This sense of security in the client will vary with the level of expertise of the worker and the personal state (level of anxiety, self-confidence, resourcefulness) of the client. Authority is always present in the worker-client relationship and the worker cannot be divested of the authority and power as he is the provider/supplier of the services the client needs. This also means, therefore, that worker-client relationship cannot be on equal terms. Power emanating from authority becomes apparent when the worker gives appointment, includes other members of the family in the treatment process, explains him the dynamics of various situations and questions his late arrival etc.

Weber, as described by Haralambos and Heald (1980), has described three types of authority as under: (i) traditional, (ii) charismatic, and (iii) legal authority.

Traditional

It is based on the belief in the rightness of customs and traditions. This perpetuates the social order and it is available to individuals and groups who inherit it from their predecessors like priests, father in the Indian family, etc.

Charismatic

This is derived from the submission (devotion) felt by the subjects to a certain man because of his special or exceptional qualities. Rama, Krishna, Buddha, Christ, Gandhiji, etc., were in this category of persons exhibiting charisma and thereby exerted charismatic authority on the masses.

Legal Authority

It emanates from the legal provisions, e.g., acts, rules, legal procedures etc. These are rational and embody the society's wider approval.

In casework, formal (legal) authority operates only in cases of probation, aftercare, home services, etc. In such settings, the caseworker derives authority mainly from the agency. Informal (traditional and charismatic) authority grows out of respect for the caseworkers in the relationship. Authority can be used (i) to persuade the client to use casework services; (ii) to instil confidence and build up self-esteem, and minimise guilt and anxiety in the clients. This is done by lawfully siding with the client, explaining the legal position and lending due support to him; (iii) in crisis situations like suicide, violence, etc., to aid the victims; (iv) for setting limits in order to relieve the client from internal or external pressures because of which he is unable to decide the nature of action he should take in the particular situation; and (v) to inculcate appropriate values in the client so that he could substitute his socially undesirable values by the desirable ones for better life. This is achieved easily when the caseworker is in position to exert more influence (authority) on the client.

In other words, effective use of authority can (i) serve as a starting point in getting the client engaged in the helping process, (ii) help in dealing with resistance, (iii) give to the client the satisfaction of identifying with a strong/adequate person, (iv) create trust and rapport quickly, (v) help in protection of clients like immature persons, children, the aged, etc., (vi) help in handling the crisis situations in the individual's life, (vii) help in removing/minimising guilt and anxiety, and (viii) give a sense of security to the client because of which he may respond better to casework treatment. *Techniques* used in such situations are advice, limit setting, coercion, reaching-out, direct intervention etc. On the other hand, authority if not property used, can cause resistance in client, poor rapport and mutual mistrust, etc. hitting at the very root of the helping process. Indian masses are found to be more responsive to an approach based on use of authority probably because of its history of feudalistic pattern of society.

Agency

Social casework is traditionally practised under the auspices of some institution, i.e., agency. This may be either private or public, large or small like hospitals, courts, social welfare departments, child guidance clinics, schools etc. The agency, according to Perlman (1957), may be either in primary or secondary settings. *Primary settings* are those which "use the methods of social casework as the major means of administering their services". *Secondary settings* use social casework services to help the individuals make use of services rendered by other professional groups like physicians in hospitals, etc. Thus, social caseworkers are the primary personnel to render services in primary settings, e.g., welfare agency or community service and family counselling centres offering casework and group work services. In secondary settings, caseworkers are to supplement the services offered by other team members. In spite of this difference, in both the settings, the caseworker tries to achieve the objectives of the agency. In both the settings, he also collaborates with others like physicians, teachers, etc., but with differing importance and utility.

The agencies have certain functions for which these are created and established. Caseworker functions in such a way that he helps the agency in achieving the stated objectives and gets linked in this process with the community. The contact and interaction between the client and worker is always with reference to these functions, objectives and values of community being carried out and executed by these agencies. Relationship develops within the purview of the agency functions which put some limitations on the use of the caseworker's services. These limitations are because of the policy of the agencies, i.e., the nature of services and activities of the agency which may help or limit the effectiveness of services. One may find such limitations very obvious in psychiatric hospitals, probation services, rescue homes, etc. Agency functions, once clear to the client, are helpful to the caseworker in helping the client to achieve what he desires through the services of agency.

Agency is a *social system*, an organisation made up of sub-units, small groups and individuals. Expectations, bureaucratic as well as professional, from the social workers (or other professionals), are source of conflict for them. Agency functioning is affected by expectations of the funding bodies, community and clientele, professionals bodies, other welfare agencies and various socio-economic forces, e.g., social and economic trends, political forces, government regulations, etc. Structure and functioning of agency are to be understood in terms of purposes, objectives and values of agency, its financial and material resources, ways of working (casework, group work, psycho-analytic approach, short-term services etc.), governing bodies, organisational structure alongwith its communication and decision-making process, staff and the clientele. To understand agency as social system one should try to understand the persons (with their attributes) influencing interactions in the agency, their roles and the influence of small groups, formal structure, and power system in decision-making in the agency.

The only departure is in the case of private practice. However, in India, no one is practising as social worker though we have many social workers practising as psychotherapist. The reasons are well known. Social workers are yet to be recognised as a professional group by the community and there is yet to be a recognised professional body to regulate education and training of social workers and to licence private practice in social work. The Association of Schools of Social Work in India is working in this direction and in all probability, a Council of Social Work Education may be formed by Government of India, the framework for which was discussed at Tata Institute of Social Sciences, Mumbai, in the month of June 1993.

Impediments to Relationship

In the interactions with the client, the worker's attitudes and prejudices may show up, all because of his living in a society where these are expressed usually without constraints. Very often, we have prejudices against certain castes, religion or region, some rituals, or some cultural beliefs. These may get expressed suddenly once the worker is not aware of it. The worker then has either to straighten these personal attitudes and behaviour patterns or to have self-control and self-awareness. Similarly aged or high caste person (worker or client) because of favourable attitudes prevailing in our society towards them, get better response. Conversely, an young or a low caste worker may have problem atleast initially because he is not considered to be capable of delivering services. Language, in our Indian settings, is a big problem because of so many languages and innumerable dialects. Communication is always hindered because of it. Diversity in cultural practices present difficulties for the worker to relate and maintain positive relationship. Worker in such diverse situations are invariably considered to be alien. These personal and cultural factors have to be controlled to be effective in relating to the client.

Apart from these factors, attitudes and feelings though uncalled for and irrational to the situation get expressed in interactions with the client. The client may express these unconsciously as a reaction to the worker in the situation as if he is a figure of the past, in other words, the worker is identified with someone in the earlier parts of the life e.g. childhood, adolescence etc. Psychoanalysis calls it *transference* which occurs in almost all the relationships. This may be helpful or unhelpful: once it is unhelpful to the growth and change of the client, it should be worked out. Sometimes, rules and policies of the agency may also impose limitations hindering proper development of relationship e.g. timings and routine of the agency, rules, facilities provided etc. may work as a barrier to the establishment of rapport. Such things happen more in institutional settings.

It can be said, then that the worker should be aware of his own emotional needs, attitudes and prejudices, values; discuss and clarify the agency practices; honestly accept limitations posed by language or lack of information about local conditions; and work out negative transference hindering proper interaction with the client.

How to Develop Relationship?

Relationship is the basis of all help. Therefore, the relationship does and should develop around the act of helping the client. Helping the client is the purpose for which interaction takes place between the worker and client which is affected by their experiences of relating with people in the past, their expectations from each other and anxieties about the situation, philosophy (values and principles of life) governing their lives, prejudices, likings and norms of behaviour, knowledge and experience about the subject matter of interaction. If we know and remain aware of these, our interaction will be more realistic. This requires training and experience in the social skill of *active awareness*. Development of relationships is also affected by the agency setting (e.g. medical settings, correctional settings, educational settings), time limits, capacities, motivations, expectations, purpose of the various units in the interaction; the nature of problem (simple, complicated, situational or personality problem, etc.) and the goals sought; and the personality make-up of the worker (maturity, helpfulness, sensitivity, courage, creativity etc.).

Necessary to develop and maintain relationship apart from the said constrains, is the worker's training in and mastery of *interpersonal skills* like active awareness, building trust, communicating, listening and expression of feelings etc. Literature is available on these and many others which can be used for training of self and as well as the clients. Acceptance of the client combined with genuineness and interest to help him is fundamental to strengthen positive relationship (rapport).

The worker should always open (start) his interviews *from where the client is* (emotionally) and from the positive side more so during the initial phases. Principles involved in establishing relationship (Biestek, 1957) are individualisation (see Chapter 2) purposeful expression of feelings (creating an atmosphere for expressing feelings freely without trying to block it by giving advice or solution with little understanding of the situation), controlled emotional response (i.e., sensitivity to the clients feelings and responding appropriately based on the understanding of the clients feelings), acceptance (see Chapter 2): non-judgemental attitude (i.e., the caseworker never tries to assign guilt or responsibility of the problem to the client, thus avoids passing judgement about the causation of the problem), right of self-determination and confidentiality (see Chapter 2 for its meaning). Empathy and communicating techniques (discussed in the chapter on Interviewing) are basic to establish and maintain relationship. Additionally, the case worker should continue to reinforce the clients motivation to work on the problem through maintaining his anxieties at a particular level reminding him of his responsibility to solve his problems and of its implications for his future and his status in society, etc.

5

Communication

Our very social existence is dependent upon the skill we have acquired and developed to communicate. One communicates in order to learn the socially approved ways of acting; to know what others think of him, what behaviour pleases or displeases those around him; and to exchange information and ideas with them. One relates, influences and develops mutual confidence only through various skills of communication.

Any breakdown in the process of communication may cause interpersonal problems, tensions, frustrations, anxieties, and in some cases, lead to some pathological manifestations. It is through the process of communication that we, as human beings, are confirmed, disconfirmed or rejected by those around us. When this process breaks down between different castes, and segments and groups of our society, violence shows up.

From the day of birth, a human being is involved in the complex process of learning the process and means of communication. Lack of communication leads us to assume that others perceive the world around us as we do, and thus we fail to understand one another. In such a situation, we often assume that the other person or group is either 'bad' or 'sick'. And this, then, may lead to interpersonal problems.

Definition and Principles of Communication

Communication involves giving or receiving a message to another individual with the conscious intent of eliciting and evoking a response and checking out its meaning. Communication refers to all behaviour, both verbal and non-verbal, which occur in a social context. Another word for communication could be 'interaction'. Fabun (1960) puts it very simply, when he says:

> "The interactions between the 'happening' that is you, and the 'happenings' that are NOT you, are the raw, basic stuff we try to communicate about."

Communication, therefore, can be through words, the way we stand, the tone of our voice, the way we look at another, i.e., any behaviour that we use to express what we are experiencing. There is a message in communication; it may be expressed verbally, non-verbally or through postures or body language.

Messages may be verbal, non-verbal or behavioural stimulus. The sender transmits the message to the receiver through a *channel* (means) like sound waves of the voice, light waves involved in seeing, printed words etc. Basic elements involved in the process of communication can be discerned as given below:

1. The intentions, ideas, feelings of the sender, and the behaviour he selects to engage in, all of which lead to his sending a message which conveys some content.
2. The sender encoding his message by translating his ideas, feelings and intentions into a message appropriate for transmission.
3. The transmission of the message to the receiver.
4. The channel through which the message is transmitted.
5. The receiver decoding the message by taking the stimuli received and interpreting its meaning. The interpretation of

the meaning of a message depends upon the receiver's comprehension of the content of the message and of the intention of the sender.

6. The receiver responding internally or externally to the interpretation of the message.

There is always some amount of noise in these steps. *Noise* is an element that interferes with the communication process. In the sender, noise can refer to such things as the attitudes, prejudices, or frame of reference of the sender and the inappropriateness of his language etc. In the receiver, it refers to such things as the attitudes, background, and experiences of the receiver which affect the decoding and interpretation. In the channel noise refers to environmental factors such as weather, or traffic, speech problems such as a tendency to fumble, or other distractions. To a large extent, the success of communication is determined by the degree to which noise is overcome or controlled. All our communications pass through these processes though we are usually not aware of it. All these steps are gone through mechanically. The principles discussed below speak about the nature of communication which if assimilated will facilitate our communication and render it effective:

1. *Communication is an interaction situation wherein the participants are affected by each one's behaviour.* Every message is simultaneously a stimulus to new behaviour and a response to prior behaviour of the receiver. No message should be isolated from what has occurred before between the communicants if we really want to understand the message. It should be understood in the totality of the situation.
2. *One does communicate.* We do communicate even when we are ignoring the message of another or maintaining complete silence. An easy way to understand this would be to think what you would do if someone, you did not want to interact with, passed a smile to you. Even by ignoring

him, you would still be communicating, "I do not want to relate to you". Silence, posture and all non-verbal behaviours are the ways we communicate even when we wish to deny doing so.

3. *The message received is not necessarily the message sent.* We usually relate to others as if there was only one reality the way we perceive the world. We all live as separate individuals with different experiences and different views of 'reality'. How we interpret verbal and non-verbal messages may be quite different from the meaning intended by the speaker (communicator). Even when several people are viewing the same behaviour, each interprets it differently. While talking or writing we are describing only those experiences that occur inside us and they may not be the same for others because every person, because of his different background, is *unique*.
4. *Communication occurs simultaneously at more than one level.* We communicate on the level of the literal content of the information being conveyed as well as on the relationship level. In other words, we do not convey information to the receiver verbally only. By the context, in which the communication occurs, and by various verbal and non-verbal cues, we are also telling the other person how we see our relationship with him, how we see ourselves, and how he should interpret our messages.

This second level of communication is called 'metacommunication' and refers to any communication about communication or any verbal or non-verbal cues about the literal content of the message sent. For example, I may say to another person, "I'm very happy with you", and be serious indicating that I do not mean what I say. I may also verbally metacommunicate by adding, "I was only joking", which tells the receiver how he should interpret my original statement.

The context in which communication occurs is another important component of metacommunication. If I slap my wife while travelling in the bus, I would be telling the world something quite different than if I were to do the same thing in my own house.

Means of Communication

An effective communication takes place when the sender transfers meaning (what he is experiencing) to the receiver; in other words, the receiver should receive exactly the same message which is being sent to him or is intended by the sender. Messages may be sent through a variety of means, both verbal and non-verbal, as explained earlier.

Communicating through Touch

As children, we all have experienced and perceived the world around us by touch. We embraced our parents, and explored the moving and coloured things around us. When angry we expressed our feelings by frowning, abusing and/or hitting. By the time we are adults, we have learned to repress much of the physical contact, we used, to express ourselves to others.

Communication of caring and openness can occur through touching. Physical contact can be reassuring, can create peace, or convey a sense of sharing, closeness, understanding, pleasure or anger. Touch can decrease the alienation of individuals from themselves and can convey feelings for another which cannot be expressed through words alone. In some instances, physical contact may be necessary before the other person can accept or hear the verbal message being sent. The feeling of closeness expressed through physical contact may dismantle the barrier erected by the other person faster than mere verbal communication.

Body Language

Body language is what our body expresses about our inner experiences. It can be the way we sit, stand, hold our head, our eyes and lips move etc. Basically, body language refers to any movement of all or part of our body which expresses an intention or emotional message to those concerned.

Body language may be either conscious or unconscious. We may scratch our palm and tap the fingers to indicate the impatience, wink to indicate intimacy, or frown to indicate displeasure. Sometimes we are aware of what we are expressing and many a time, it is purely an unconscious reaction to our inner state. Often, the feelings expressed through our body do not get expressed verbally and may even be in conflict with our verbal statements. For these reasons, it is extremely important that we are aware of what message we are sending to others through our body.

Use of Symbols

When one uses words (symbols) for communication, the meaning is not in the word, but in the person who uses it. Words are *self-selected symbols* chosen to represent a particular experience. They have little meaning in themselves. Forgetting the abstract nature of words (i.e., the words in themselves have no meaning) is an important cause of failure to communicate properly and adequately.

Each commonly used word covers a wide variety of meanings, because each of them is used by millions of people in a variety of ways. The meaning attributed to a particular word will vary from individual to individual. What the phrase "bit late" means to one person may be quite different than what it means to another. We all have experienced that there are some inner states which are totally indescribable through words alone. No language is capable of describing all our experiences adequately. 'गिरा अनयन नयन बिनु बाणी' (Tulsi's Rāmāyan) expresses this limitation by telling that speech does not have eyes and eyes have no speech to describe what they experience or perceive.

The symbols (words) used by us limit us in what we are able to think and express. We look for things for which we have words to describe, and if there are no words for a certain experience, we tend to ignore it or use a word or phrase which may approach, but not exact the feeling.

We organise what we perceive according to the structure of our language. For example, think of many of our adjectives such as good-bad, beautiful-ugly, smart-dumb, bright-dull, and then try to think of words to describe something in between good or bad. It is because of our language structure that many of us tend to see and describe the world as an "either-or"

Johnson (1951) points out how each profession's language causes them to look for certain things for which they have words to describe, and to ignore others. His conclusion is that if we are to improve our ability to understand others, we must learn, all the special language we can, from the language of neurology, anatomy, Freud, Pavlov, to the language of general semantics. In this way, we will be able to organise and evaluate our experience more effectively and have a better understanding of the individuals in interaction with us and the world around us.

In addition to words, we also use visible means such as painting or sculpture to send messages. All of these are real events that are experienced and interpreted by us just as other real events are.

Sending Clear Messages

All communications though 'good', are by its very nature incomplete. This section will explore some typical problems we face in sending clear messages.

During childhood most of us were probably fairly direct in expressing our needs through touch or physical contact and body language. When we were hungry, we cried and asked for food. Even as we learned to talk, we continued to be open and would say directly to someone we did not like, "I don't want you here". However, as we got older, we learnt that it was often risky to express exactly what we were experiencing towards another. We learned that it was not proper to say certain things and learned to distrust our own inner experience and to depend on others to tell us what was good, bad, or acceptable. As a result, we learned to 'encode' our messages in various forms and thereby protect ourselves against possible rejection, punishment or loss of affection.

There are a variety of ways in which we may send encoded messages. We may not acknowledge ownership of our feelings, thoughts, or behaviour. "We all feel that way", "You are making me feel bad", or "You are making me angry" are the ways of expressing ourselves which places the responsibility for our thoughts and feelings on someone, 'you' or 'we'. These general 'you' or 'we' messages protect us from directly expressing our own feelings and put the blame on someone or something else, or dilute the personal responsibility for the messages.

Another common error in sending clear messages is the failure to distinguish between fact and opinion. We assume that our perception of a person or thing is the correct perception. Sentences like "picture is ugly", "she is repulsive", or "he is really selfish" mean that we assume that the ugliness, repulsiveness and selfishness exist independently of our personal experience of it. In reality, we are describing an internal experience which is valid for us only. Pictures are not 'ugly', we experience them as 'ugly'. It is not a fact, rather it is our perception of the person or situation.

Most of the above errors in sending clear messages can be avoided by using the word 'I' and by documenting our statements like, "I feel angry because you did not turn up there", "I find her selfish because she did not lend her pen for one day", "I feel bad about what you are saying because you have not verified the facts", etc.

Contradictory Messages

Overgeneralising, anecdotes, apologies, not coding our messages in words familiar to the receiver, and sending several messages at one time are the characteristics of poor communicating.

Another common error is to send contradictory messages, i.e., where two or more messages sent on the same level contradict one another. For example, we may say, "Go away... No, don't leave me", or "I'm very angry at you... No, I'm not". In this situation, it is relatively apparent to the receiver that the communicator is confused. He may ask directly, "What do you really mean?"

Incongruent Messages

When two or more contradictory messages are sent on different levels, we are sending what is called incongruent messages. For example, I may say, "Go away", and then hold the person physically. I am verbally communicating that he may go away but the non-verbal or metacommunication is that I want him to come closer. We often send incongruent messages because we are not comfortable in the situation. While receiving the incongruent messages, the receiver may depend upon the metacommunication to interpret what the other person means to convey.

When we send incongruent messages, we are often seen as untrustworthy by the receiver. Rogers (1954), in his writings, points out the importance of being seen as real or congruent. What he wishes to refer is that verbal communication should be consistent with the metacommunication. Those in the helping professions sometimes have the impression that they are to be all accepting and impartial and are not to experience or express negative feelings about anything a client says or does. Consequently, when we are angry at a client, we tend to repress these feelings and are unaware that these are in fact being communicated to the client through our body language. Therefore, one should be honest enough to accept it and explain the reasons for experiencing or metacommunicating the negative feelings.

Feedback

Feedback is used to know how we are affecting others and if we are sending any contradictory message. Feedback refers to conscious communication, giving informations as to how we are affecting others, or in other words, how others in the situation feel or think of the action of the person (actor).

To increase our self-awareness feedback should be specific and documented by examples of behaviour which has preferably just occurred, i.e., feedback should focus on behaviour not on the person. Feedback received should correspond to what the sender had in mind. It should be based on observations and not on inferences. Similarly, it is effective when it is based on description of behaviour rather than on judgement. For example, Mrs. A congratulates Mrs. B on receiving Ph.D. If Mrs. B tells Mrs. A that her face looked tense while congratulating her, this will be feedback, but if she says that Mrs. A was unhappy over her getting Ph.D., it will be interpretation and not feedback.

Double-level Messages

When communication and metacommunication contradict one another, it is called an incongruent message. An even more complicated situation emerges when the verbal and non-verbal metacommunication conflict. If we say, "Go away", then pull the person back, and then say, "I don't want you here", we are sending what is called double-level message. The receiver can no longer depend on the metacommunication to help him interpret the message because the verbal and non-verbal metacommunication also conflict.

The effects of this kind of interaction were first described by a group of researchers while studying the communication of schizophrenics. This group approached it by asking themselves what kind of interpersonal experience would induce the bahaviour of a schizophrenia in a person. They found certain communication patterns existing in families of schizophrenics and termed these patterns "double-bind messages", i.e., two conflicting communications from the sender, when one message is usually verbal and the other is non-verbal.

There are several conditions which are necessary before a double-bind message can affect the person seriously. These are described as under:

First, the double-level messages must occur frequently and over a long period of time.

Secondly, these must be sent by someone who has control over the receiver. This often occurs in families where parents send such messages to their children who are dependent on them for food, protection and love. However, it may also occur in other high intensity relationships.

Thirdly, the receiver must be forbidden to check out the intended message but must take all the conflicting cues and try to make sense of them. Frequently, the sender also strongly indicates that the receiver should show no awareness of any contradiction between various messages, and he may be punished for attempting to do so. The crux of a double-bind message is that by obeying one message the recipient is disobeying the other. He is damned if he does and also if he doesn't.

Some examples of double-bind messages are: (1) a father demands that his son stand up to him like a man and yet punishes him when he does so, or (2) a family insists that their child be upright and honest and yet praise him when he takes others for a ride.

Receiving Messages

Sending a message is only the beginning of the process of communication. Valid communication does not occur until the receiver has received the intended message of the sender. This is accomplished by the recipient interpreting the message and checking this interpretation with the sender.

We receive messages through the same basic means that are used by the sender to transmit his experience: through physical contact, body language, verbal content, and the context in which the communication occurs. Although we are usually unaware of it, all our five senses of touch, sight, hearing, taste and smell may be engaged in helping us to give meaning to the speaker's messages.

Interpreting and Evaluating Messages

We try to understand others through our own interpretation system which depends upon our ability to perceive needs and wishes of others. As stated above, we take in the data through our five senses. We hear, taste, smell, feel and see some behaviour in the other person. All this data then go through our own private 'computer', and we attribute some meaning to it. The meaning we give to it is based on our prior experience with other people and on our particular expectations of the sender—how we have seen him react to us or to other people before. For example, I find someone standing in front of me with a gun raised and pointed directly at me and with a scowl on his face. I recognise him and know from my prior experience that he likes me. I think it all a joke and that he has no intentions of killing me. In the same situation, when the person is an enemy, the meaning we would make of the same data would be quite different because of my prior experience and relationship with him.

Once we have taken in the data, it has gone through our computer, and we have decided what this data means to us, the next step in our internal process is to experience feelings accordingly. We are only partially aware of these feelings and we rarely verbalise it to another. However, we communicate feelings to others mostly through our body language. We may show guilt by pulling ourselves back, lowering our head or shifting our glance. All these non-verbal cues tell the speaker our unconscious reaction to his statements. Our reactions are partially dependent upon our state of mind (mood) at the particular moment. Certain behaviours on the part of the speaker may cause us to became defensive, i.e., to protect or justify ourselves. If I feel the other person is evaluating me, feels superior, or is trying to control me, I may become less and less able to perceive his motives accurately. Our own needs may take precedence over any message that he is sending.

In addition to the body language, one may also take a conscious action in response to the sender's message. I may say, "Stop boring me", or "I do not want to talk about it now". In so doing 'I' become sender of a new message, and the communication process continues. In addition to being aware of our own interpretation system, we also need to get in touch with what the message means to the sender. An important step in getting in touch with other's feelings is to never be dogmatic about how he feels. We cannot afford to assume that because of our training or vast experience, we can tell exactly what another is transmitting to us about his personal experience.

Active Listening

'Active listening' is a concept developed by Rogers (1966) in his client-centered therapy. In active listening, we listen to what the person is saying, both the content and feelings expressed and we verbally acknowledge that we are hearing him. Our primary purpose is not to check out to see if we have received the intended message but rather to let him know that we are listening to and understanding what he is expressing.

In active listening, we only rephrase the statements of the sender. We do not evaluate, give our own opinion, advice, or interpret. We continue active listening until the speaker indicates either verbally or non-verbally that he has stopped speaking for the time being. For example:

Anju: While I was objecting to his coming late for dinner, he pushed me into the bed.

Th: You mean he got angry.

Anju: Yes, he got angry and wanted to stop me.

Th: He wanted to stop you.

Active listening lets the sender know what I am hearing and that I am accepting his message and he is also encouraged to say more and more and to share his feelings. As he continues to talk and feel accepted and comfortable, he moves away from presenting problem to his deeper feelings. He becomes more aware of and gains new insights into his behaviour and feelings.

Active listening cannot be applied equally to all situations. For instance, if someone requests information about the location of a place etc., he probably will not appreciate if the response is like "You would really like to know where this place is?" It is up to the receiver to decide from verbal or non-verbal cues whether the person wants to pursue the subject or not.

In a nutshell, we can be effective in communication when we learn and practise to (1) repeat the message, (2) use more than one channel, (3) specify and complete the messages, (4) own responsibility for our feelings, and (5) be congruent in our verbal and non-verbal communications. In all the helping professions, much of what we do is based on our ability to communicate effectively. An understanding of the basic premises of human communication and some of the common errors in sending or receiving of messages is essential. Hopefully, through increasing our awareness of ourselves, and of how we affect others, and by developing skills in interpreting what another is expressing to us, we can enhance our capacity to communicate in both our professional and day-to-day life.

6

Interviewing and Recording

It is through the relationship that we help the client(s) and this relationship in turn is dependent upon our communication, both verbal and non-verbal. No doubt, non-verbal communication is more meaningful than verbal; it occurs only when attempts are made to have verbal interaction with the clients. The verbal interaction, i.e., interviewing, is guided and affected by the view of roles and needs of the client, purpose of the interview and the personalities of the worker and client. It is through this interviewing process only that the client is understood, his needs are assessed and a plan of action is formulated and implemented. The image of the social caseworker will be very much dependent upon the experience the client has in the interviewing sessions.

What is interviewing? It is "communicating with a conscious purpose". Kahn and Connell (1957) define interviewing as a "specialised pattern of verbal interaction initiated for a specific purpose, focused on specific content area, with consequent elimination of extraneous material". Herein, the roles of the client and worker are quite specific and dependent upon the purpose. Thus, interviewing has (1) specific context in which the verbal interaction takes place, (2) purpose which gives a direction to the interviewing process, (3) a limit with explicit or implied contract between the worker and client, and (4) a specialised role relationship.

The social caseworker's interviews differ from non-therapeutic interviews in terms of techniques, self-awareness, professional norms and values, therapeutic commitments and objectives, agency's purpose and policies, and the specific roles.

The interviewer is the 'leader' or the person who has agency's (community's) sanction to act in the capacity of a 'helper'. It should be noted that not all interviews are helping interviews; people can meet together for purposes other than working together to solve a problem, e.g., correspondents, investigators, etc. An interview then can be used as a tool to get or give information, or, it can be used as a process in which growth and change of all the participants occur. It is the latter type which is characteristic of social work interviews.

There are four aspects which have been identified by many writers as essential to the successful helping interviews. These, related to the worker's behaviour, are:

1. individual honesty
2. empathy
3. non-possessive warmth
4. unconditional acceptance

These have already been discussed in the chapter on communication. The interviews pass through at least three stages: initial, middle and termination. The initial stage assumes importance because of its value for establishing relationship—the basis for all help. The initial phase of contact between an interviewer and his client(s) is often fraught with anxiety and apprehension for the people involved. This happens, it seems, due to the client's lack of clarity about expectations, responsibilities, and purpose as well as his real question as to whether or not this contact or series of contacts will be helpful. The first task of the interviewer is then to help create a relaxed and informal and productive atmosphere in which he and his client(s) can begin to work followed by explanation of roles, purpose and plan. We can now discuss some of the steps necessary to create such an atmosphere.

The Setting

The setting for the interviewing should be quiet, uncluttered, and as attractive and comfortable as possible. Avoid interruptions if the interview is held at a private place like home etc.

Verbalising the Feelings

To be helpful, an interviewer must be aware of the feelings, in particular, the negative and uncomfortable feelings, both in himself and his client. He must be attuned to the non-verbal behaviour of the client(s) as well as to his own bodily sensations. This is possible only when the worker learns to listen which involves receiving verbal as well as non-verbal message communicated by the client. He must then verbalise his own feelings and help the client(s) to do so. The principles, to start where the client is and acceptance are to be kept in view while opening the interview. He might say, for example:

"I find that you are sitting very tight (or your hands are clenched, or you're sweating etc.). How do you feel sitting like this?"

"It is often hard to come to an unknown person to ask for help. I find that I'm a bit nervous in this situation and I wonder if you too are."

Throughout the interview situation, it is essential for the interviewer to be as open, honest, clear and direct as possible. In verbalising his own feelings, the interviewer sets the tone for future contacts. In being able to take risk by exposing himself, the interviewer implicitly allows and helps the client(s) to do so as well.

Making Explicit the Purpose of the Interview

As explained earlier, interview moves in the desirable direction only when its purpose is made clear. Therefore, the persons initiating contact should tell others the purpose of the interview. If the interviewer has initiated the contact, he should explain the purpose of the interview as directly as possible. While on a home visit, one may say, "We are concerned that Suketu has been missing school for long", rather than that "I was just in the neighbourhood and I thought I'd stop and chat".

When the contact has been initiated by the client, the interviewer should allow the client time and latitude in stating his reasons for requesting the interview. If the client needs help in getting started, the interviewer may ask a neutral question about the client's purpose, expectations or hopes about the contact. Expectations of the client should be discussed thoroughly so that his unrealistic expectations do not throttle the helping process. While removing his apprehensions and clarifying his doubts and straightening his expectations, care should be taken to maintain the motivation level of the client, failing which he will leave coming to seek help.

The interviewer should not assume that he knows what is on the client's mind even if he has seen the client before, read the case record, or has spoken to others about him for simple reason that the client may come out with something new and his tone and expressions will acquaint the worker with the seriousness of the problem. Also, asking about and helping the client to talk about his reasons for initiating the contact allows the interviewer to understand the client's feelings and perceptions of self *vis-à-vis* his situations.

Clarifying the Helping Process

In the initial interview and often during the first few interviews, the interviewer and client(s) must come to a clear understanding of the purpose of interacting together. The following aspects are to be included in the initial contacts:

(a) Statement of the problems to be considered during the interviews.
(b) Statement of the goals. If the goals of the interviewer and client(s) are not the same initially, they must be discussed until an agreement is reached which is acceptable to all concerned.
(c) Clarification of responsibility, i.e., those things which the interviewer will do and those which the client(s) will do. In general, it is the client's responsibility to bring for consideration anything which he would like to discuss in the interview and to act upon the discussions outside the interview. It is the responsibility of the interviewer to conduct the discussion in such a way as to make it a purposeful and productive interaction in terms of the agreed upon goals.
(d) Statement of the time, frequency and length of interview.
(e) Decision about the method of intervention (e.g., individual interviews, small group meetings, intervention in community system etc.)

One should not think that the interaction is a static subject dictated by one or the other parties. Rather, it has to be fluid and responsive to the needs, hopes and expectations of both the interviewer and the client. Throughout the course of intervention (treatment), the nature of contact, its purpose, etc., may be rediscussed as and when goals or situations change. Interviewer and client must be free to discuss various aspects of the interaction. *Discussion* on the said lines is possible only in the cases of well-educated clients. Most of cases in Indian settings require clarification about the nature of help agency/worker can extend. Formality about timing etc. is likely to create misunderstanding because of our informal and warm social life. Knowledge of local socio-cultural patterns is always beneficial.

The initial phase of contacts between interviewer and client(s) may be relatively easy or quite difficult. The interviewer may need to "reach out" to the clients in an assertive yet accepting way so that the contacts are initiated. This might entail some or all of the following:

1. Going out to meet the clients at their own homes, schools, jobs or recreation areas.
2. Verbalising the differences in lifestyle, culture, etc., which might block communication or which the client may expect to block communication.
3. Making oneself available at a time or a schedule different than that usually followed.
4. Utilising the help of other persons significant to the client's problem-solution.

These signify the worker's interest in the client's welfare and solution of his problems.

The mistakes commonly indulged in by interviewers, specially by the inexperienced ones, enumerated below, lead to blocking of communication between the worker and client:

1. *Reassuring too soon*: "You will be alright soon." "No problem, it will be solved soon." These sentences show that the interviewer is feeling insecure and does not want to explore the feelings and the reasons for it. Thus, this assurance blocks further communication.
2. *Explaining quickly*: Many times, we try to explain (or justify) how and why the father did not allow the client to go on pleasure trip without responding to and exploring the feelings of the client. The hidden message is that I have no time to waste for you (client) or I cannot stand your (client's) irrelevant talks.
3. *Bossing over*: "Tell me all about your problems if you want to be helped." Here, the interviewer shows his indifference to the feelings and reactions of the client towards the worker and helping process. The message is that you are getting heavy on me. This approach however, may be useful in history taking in medical and psychiatric settings.

4. *Responding too quickly*: "I know what you want to say. I know you are feeling bad." The message is that I am not interested to hear you.
5. *Interpreting quickly*: "I know you hate your father because..." "You are angry with me because I told you..." The message is that I am getting impatient with your (client's) feelings.
6. *Advising too soon*: "I think you should meet... and discuss it. It will solve your problems." The message is that I have no patience to hear the details. I want to get rid of you. I am too expert to deal with such problems.

The interviewer must explore the feelings and reactions of the client before reacting to it and should check his all such behaviours which discourage communication.

The caseworker should

(a) question the client's statements, like "I have been always doing like this," "I have always been like this". These statements are excuses to avoid discussion and efforts to change one's way of behaving;
(b) listen to the client to understand what is really being said;
(c) avoid taking over responsibility of the client. Work as enabler so that the client solves his problems on his own; and
(d) focus on the present situation and explore the possible alternatives to change the situation. Historical reasons or excuses, if given, should be worked through.

Interviewing Techniques

We shall now discuss the specific interviewing techniques used in social casework practice.

Exploration

It starts with questions about age etc. and proceeds to explore the client's feeling and experiences with open-ended questions.

According to Thomas et al (1960), if the worker is uncertain as to why the client is emphasising a particular thing, or taking a question, or making a request, complaint, accusation, and so forth, it is wise to make further inquiry as to just what the client has in mind, and why it is important to him. Exploring through questioning and commenting is also useful when the worker wants clients to look in more depth at a certain subject. This helps in collecting relevant data for diagnostic purposes and may lead the client to think various unexplored areas of the problem, thus helping him to have insight into the problem.

Would you mind explaining...?
Would you tell me more about that...?
What kind of things you think...?
What do you mean by...?
Could you give me an example of...?
Can you tell me how...happened?
I think you mean that...?

Ventilation

It means helping a client to express strong feelings when he may be hesitant to do so because of his uncertainty regarding the worker's response, or because he simply does not have the words to express these feelings. Verbalising feelings by a client permits understanding of his emotional state. Once the client is free from the possessing feelings, he can clearly think through the problems and his perception of the reality gets sharpened.

Do you want to tell about...?
Are you saying you feel that...?
You seem to be uneasy about...

Topical Shift

The worker purposely changes the subject of discussion perhaps because he thinks the topic under discussion is unproductive, a blind alley, or the client is telling a sensitive matter at present, etc.

That's important, but first, could we get back to...
Before we move on to that, it might be helpful to think about...
Perhaps we have covered that enough for now, how about you mentioned...

Logical Reasoning

The worker tries to involve the client in a systematic and rational analysis of a situation that requires a decision. He should encourage the client to weigh alternative responses and to predict the possible consequences of each of the responses.

We can think about it together. If you did...
What do you think, would happen?
We can take these one at a time. Why do you think that it happens the way it does?

Encouragement

It is done through expressing confidence in the client's abilities, recognising his achievements and expressing pleasure in his successes as we do when someone gets distinction in the examination or wins a match. It is useful with children and adults lacking self-confidence or with persons in critical situation. Like any other technique, encouragement should also be based on facts and not on false premises. False encouragement is detrimental to the growth of individual. Examples are congratulating someone when successful in some competition, or when something has been achieved.

Informing

This involves informing the clients theoretically about various aspects of the situation, procedures involved in administration of services, giving knowledge about various developmental phases and behaviour characteristic of certain ages and situation etc. This removes unnecessary apprehension and instils self-confidence in the client by allaying his anxiety resulting from lack of information about and resultant misperception of the situation. For example, one can tell the parents about normal behaviour of adolescents to relieve them of unnecessary anxieties.

Generalisation (Universalisation)

This technique is used to minimise guilt or anxiety feelings in the client by generalising the nature of events or reactions; for example, one can say, "every child masturbates during adolescent period; we all feel the same way in the situation you are passing through". In effect it tells the client that his feelings and reactions are universal and normal to the situation, therefore, he need not feel guilty or anxious about these events and/or reactions.

Partialisation

In the initial phase one may try to focus on only one aspect of the total problem instead of tackling the whole problem, i.e., focusing on only one part of the problem. In choosing one part of the problem, one should be careful to see that the part problem chosen is of immediate importance to him and can be solved with the available resources in the shortest possible time. Once his immediate worries are tackled, it will strengthen the relationship between the worker and client and increase the client's respect for the worker.

Explaining

This technique is used for helping the client to understand the situation or events in its various aspects with possible implications for the clients. The worker tries to put all the aspects of the situation/event in detail and in proper sequence to enable the client to have better intellectual understanding and appreciation of the situation/event. This helps him to take proper decision and allays his apprehensions and corrects misperception. Sometimes one may take the help of theoretical knowledge also.

Reassurance

It is used to allay unrealistic anxiety, guilts and apprehensions and create a sense of security in the client. The strength of reassurance depends upon the confidence the client has in the worker. The way the worker conducts himself in the situation can itself be reassuring to the client. His fantasies/irrational thinking can be discussed to show their baselessness, thus making the client comfortable and secure. For example, in the interview for jobs, the worker can explain the whole situation and thus make him believe that he had equal chance to be selected alongwith others and that his apprehensions about the interview board are baseless. Reassurance should be given only when the facts justify it. To cite an example, one may assure an anxious patient to be operated that there is every likelihood of its being successful. If someone tells him that the operation is bound to be successful, he is taking risk as one can never be fully sure of the operation's success. Insecure persons may seek unconditional reassurance, which should be avoided for obvious reasons.

Middle Phase

Phases of interviewing assume significance only when we see them from the focal point of view. It is the emphasis only that varies in the initial, middle and closing (termination) phases. In the middle stage of interview, the worker after establishing rapport and gathering data, tries to examine various problems, gains insight into the real problem to develop various feasible solutions, and helps the client to implement these solutions.

Finally, there are certain areas about which many clients find it hard to communicate. Negative feelings and sex are among these areas. Clients readily pick up cues from interviewers that these indeed are forbidden subjects and thus do not discuss them even though it would be appropriate within the context of the helping interview. The interviewer must become aware of his own feelings about these and other difficult subjects and must become comfortable with them. He also must be aware of the client's needs to discuss these and help him to verbalise them.

Though there is no hard and fast rule as to which technique should be used in what phase of the interview, one can say that the following techniques are used more often in the middle phase of the interview. These techniques are:

Externalisation of Interest

In this technique, the client is guided to explore his interest in various hobbies (arts, crafts, games, etc.) available to him. His interest is aroused in these activities so that his preoccupation with his inner problems is offset by it and he maintains touch with the outside world. He is persuaded to undertake some hobby which will engage his attention and involve his thinking also.

Individualisation

This is just opposite to generalisation. Herein, the client is made to feel that the reactions/feelings are unique to the client and he should own responsibility for it if he is to solve his problem. This is required in those cases where the client avoids taking responsibility for his feelings/reactions by generalising it. One may say, for example, "I think, Mr. X, it is you who feel like this. Others do not feel like this in such situations."

Resource Utilisation

It is a very common technique of social casework which implies that all the resources available to the client, including interpersonal as well as community resources, are used to help the client and protect his legitimate interest. In this process, one can use the resources of friends, relatives, neighbours, public and private agencies, in addition to his own (client's) intelligence, physique, education, talents, etc., to help him to solve his problem and adjust to his environment.

Limit-setting

This involves checking the behaviour/activities of the client at a particular point because allowing him to act beyond that point will be detrimental to the client's interest. This can be achieved through use of authority or by shift of topics of discussion during the interview. Examples: "I think we have discussed this for long and now we will discuss... I don't think we can discuss this because..."

Confrontation

Herein the client is confronted with his own motor behaviour, feelings, reactions etc. These are brought to his attention in its various aspects to help him to understand his own reactions to the situation/event/person. This brings in insight necessary for effecting desirable change in his approach to deal with life situations. Examples: "You remember your eyes got red and your voice got raised when I...You remember you said 'No' when I requested you to see your hospitalised brother."

Clarification

This involves clarifying the reality as distinct and separate from fantasy. This seeks to correct distorted ideas that are unrealistic. This helps in developing awareness of unproductive repetitious behaviour patterns and of the ego defenses operating in individual's such behaviour patterns. Herein, the client is made aware of certain attitudes and feelings colouring his reality perception; once he is aware of it, he can see how his actions are against his own real interests. His awareness of his own attitudes and feelings helps him to see the situation objectively. He thus develops better control and takes decision according to his real needs and existing reality. Examples: "How do you know that your father-in-law is angry with you? How can you say that college-going girls do not make good wives? Can you secure first division in the examination by studying for one hour daily only?"

Interpretation

It is meaning (why) of the client's behaviour in terms of the influence of his earlier experiences with parents and siblings on his current functioning. The current functioning is interpreted in terms of his experiences in childhood and he is made to realise that his own actions are against his own interest. Interpretation of the reaction of the client is done in terms of how (dynamic functioning) also, i.e., in terms of interaction between thinking and feelings, ego, id and superego, defense mechanisms and impulses etc. Examples: "Are you afraid of your boss because you were afraid of your father? Do you fulfil all the wishes of your wife irrespective of its cost because of your domineering sex urges."

Terminal Stage

Time at which an individual interview is to be concluded, in most cases, should be decided in advance. As part of the understanding, the length and frequency of interview should be decided and this should be observed fully. This may create some problem with the clients coming from low socio-economic status as well as from poorly educated families. Often, in an attempt to prolong the interview, a client will bring up a very important matter during the last minutes of the interview. The decision about whether to allow the discussion or to close the interview on schedule, must depend, in part, on the nature of the material, an assessment of the client's motivation for bringing it up so late and whether or not this is characteristic behaviour of the client.

The decision to end the interactions is the one which must be made jointly by the helper and the client. Some of the following considerations should be included in the decisions:

1. Have some or all of the goals been met? To what extent?
2. Do the interviewer and the clients feel this is an appropriate time to end?
3. What more can or should the client do on his own?

It is best to discuss termination and its ramifications several times before the final interview. Often it is helpful to taper off the frequency of interviews in order to give the client(s) experience in handling things alone for greater length of time. Recorded interviews (on cassette recorder) are helpful to reinforce the effects of casework if these are repeatedly heard by the client after the termination of the helping process.

Termination of the helping process brings up in both the interviewer and client(s) many feeling—both positive and negative—which must be verbalised and discussed.

Summarising

A preferred technique is to summarise briefly major issues or conclusions at the end of an interview. This serves as a review for interviewer and client(s), as a method of clarifying misunderstood points and as a place from where to begin the next interview.

In terminating a series of contacts, summarising is a tool to assess movement, growth and change. As such, it serves as a source of hope for the future.

The client and the therapist should discuss the possibility of renewed contacts in the future if it should become necessary. This is important so that the client does not feel completely alone and if it becomes necessary, can re-initiate contacts without losing face.

Skills in Social Casework

Skill is the capacity to perform a task or act in such a way that the objectives are realised effectively and within the shortest possible time. Skill development depends upon training, practice, experience and knowledge of human behaviour. Basically, there are four skills required for effective casework practice: (i) skill in relationship, (ii) skill in exploring problems in depth, (iii) skill in the use of the resources, and (iv) skill in finding out alternative solutions.

Skill in Relationship

It has been discussed earlier in the chapter on relationship that casework treatment (intervention) is carried through relationship between the client and caseworker. This needs creating an atmosphere of trust, confidence and mutual respect wherein the client feels comfortable to express himself and asks for help. Skill lies in showing respect, and genuine interest in the client and his problems, respecting his opinions and values, and involving him in every stage of finding solution of his problems.

Skill in Exploring Problems in Depth

The caseworker ought to possess skills in probing the details and developmental sequence of the problem. Caseworker's ability to help the client to tell his story and to identify his real problem requires capacity to listen to, express interest and show respect to the client's versions alongwith understanding of human behaviour in different conditions, and of social conditions and human problems. Obviously, this requires capacity to empathise with the client.

Skill in the Use of Resources

Very often, services and material resources are used as tools to help the client to solve his problems. Therefore, caseworker needs capacity to tap all such resources either available in the friends circle or with the relatives or in the community of the client in general to help him. Caseworker's skill lies in locating and using these resources for helping the client in such a way that it does not damage his self-image, specially in our Indian settings.

Skill in Finding out Alternative Solutions

After having established a congenial relationship, explored his problems and tapped the needed resources, it is extremely important to discuss the possible approaches to solve the problem in greater detail and with full clarity. Alternative courses of action need to be thrashed out vividly and concretely in terms of its advantages, disadvantages, implications for everyone likely to be affected by this decision. Skill lies in helping the client to understand each alternative with its all implications and to decide for the best possible course of action in the situation. The suggested actions have to be according to his capacity, status, resources and community norms.

Home Visits

The importance of family has been well recognised by the personnel in social work, specially those in the mental health field. Study of the emotional, social and physical aspects of family life is necessary to plan the treatment effectively. It is also very important to gather sufficient details of information so that our prediction has less chance of being based on hunches or prejudices, and this is achieved easily and effectively through home visits.

Home visits aim at therapeutic, sustaining and preventive measures as well. At the WHO European Conference on Mental Hygiene Practice (1959) it was recommended that home visits should be used for diagnostic purposes, as well as for treatment and supervision of long-term patients in their own homes.

Bernard (1964) states that by making home visits one sees the environment in which the patient lives, observes family and other relevant social interactions at first hand and develops a fuller diagnostic understanding of the patient for appropriate treatment planning. Home visit has thus become an effective tool in total treatment (intervention) programme.

In the following paragraphs the purposes of home visits are described:

Getting Detailed Information about the Client and his Family

In medical and psychiatric setting, it is often impossible for the psychiatrists or the psychologists to obtain an adequate picture of the family background by interviewing the child, the parents and others concerned in the clinic. At best, according to Yapp (1959), such a method is laborious, uncertain, and may involve many interviews and a gradual piecing together of the various contributions, and at worst there is a risk of undermining the child's confidence in the therapist.

On the other hand, according to Cameron (1961), "in a few minutes in home, an experienced observer can gain more pertinent information about the patient and his environment than can be gained during hours of probing in an office." Home visits help a great deal in assessing the

(a) problems of the child, and the relevance of family interaction to these problems;
(b) personality characteristics of the parents and siblings and studying the patterns of intra-familial, interpersonal relationships; and
(c) socio-economic status of the family and the pattern of interaction with the external world.

Persuading the Patients to Utilise the Services to the Maximum Extent

In my experience with the clients of the Child Guidance Clinic, it was often observed that patients do not turn up after one or two visits to the clinic. On further investigation, one gets the impression that they lack motivation to get themselves (or their wards) treated. This lack of motivation results in their not using the therapeutic resources adequately. So, the home visits in such cases will help in adequately motivating the patient and family for seeking treatment.

Educating the Family Members in Matters of Health and Illness and for Allaying Anxiety of Relatives

The relatives of the patients harbour many wrong notions about various services including medical and psychiatric treatment mainly because of lack of knowledge. The social worker can play a significant role in educating the public in matters of various illnesses and their treatment through home visits and can allay their irrational fears and remove misconceptions etc.

Strengthening Ties Between the Client in the Institution and Family

According to David (1965), pre-release home visit by the social worker strengthens the ties between the patient and his family that are often strained to the breaking point, or it prevents further deterioration in the relationship. The home visits also help in preparing the family to receive the clients after discharge from the institution.

Facilitating Rehabilitation of the Discharged Clients from Institutions

Sheeley (1962), in an address to the New Nexico Medical Society, quoted Bourestom that the patient's failure to make a community adjustment was more apt to be due to community hostility than to continuing mental illness (or the problem). Home visits help in bringing this to the notice of the relatives and helping them in resolving the same. In addition, the family members may be counselled on reorienting their attitude to the clients and their problems so as to facilitate rehabilitation.

Family Therapy and Aftercare Services to the Discharged Patients

Ferriera and Winter (1965), on the basis of their clinical impressions derived from family therapy and the results of a handful of experiments, have come to the conclusion that the family of an individual patient is an abnormal one, different in someways from normal families. This conviction has led the workers in mental health field to include the whole family in treatment, if the patient is to be treated successfully. May et al (1962) have also found that home visits with support and advice to the family and relatives or anyone else in the immediate environment is a factor of major importance in the treatment of psychiatric patients.

There are many patients, who after extensive treatment and hospitalisation, are discharged either unimproved or slightly improved. Such patients may derive benefit from casework services in collaboration with the psychiatrist. Casework services in such cases are best rendered at homes since it has been recognised that the effect of normal home environment greatly enhances all therapeutic efforts. Home visits also enable the worker to bring about the necessary changes in those aspects of the family life and parental attitudes and behaviour which are responsible for the difficulties of the patients as well as clients discharged from institutions in correctional setting. Also, there are many who need help but would not visit the agency on their own. So, home visit appears to be the only way to approach (reaching out) such cases.

Marfatia et al (1963) used home visits for the purpose of *follow-up* and found that in majority of the cases, the improvement at discharge was maintained or increased. Colewell and Post (1963) point out that only one of a number of their ex-patients with whom the psychiatric social worker has been able to keep up regular contact after discharge had to be re-admitted during the period (two years) under review. In fact, the purpose of institutionalisation is defeated without *rehabilitative* services. The home visits enable the social worker to help the client to find a congenial home and restore his old status in the community.

Discussing the problems of the client with the leader of the team is the first step in planning the home visit. The worker should take care not to impose his own judgements, values, prejudices, etc., on the client. However, the worker should not be too formal in his behaviour. Informality in the relationship, interest in helping the patients and his family, and genuinely respecting the patient and his family in spite of his handicaps will enhance the usefulness of home visits. The language of communication should be such that the patient and his family members understand it without difficulty.

Home visits are particularly valuable in the treatment of (1) emotional problems of children and adolescents, (2) habit disorders and conduct disorders in childhood and adolescence, (3) educational problems, (4) delinquency and other behavioural disorders in children, (5) social maladjustment, (6) psychoneuroses, and (7) difficulties in family adjustment.

Referral

Sometimes, before termination, cases are referred to another caseworker or therapist like group worker in the same or to other agency for some important reasons. This is a process by which client is enabled to become aware of other services and use them.

In referral, the helping process does not end but it is the contact with a particular caseworker which terminates. The client starts a new helping relationship with another therapist. Referral is done for various considerations: (i) when a different type of worker/therapy is required to achieve the finally formulated goals of treatment, and (ii) when the worker and the client find it difficult to move to or assume new responsibility. The case may be referred to some other agency if, at some point, it is decided that the client cannot be helped in this agency for some reason, like lack of required services, etc. Referral involves preparation of a *referral note* which gives a very brief summary of the problem and the efforts undertaken to solve the problem alongwith psycho-social diagnosis.

Preparation for referral should be done in the way preparation for termination is undertaken though referral stage is not the final stage. Preparation involves (i) explaining the reasons for referral, (ii) talking of the positive and negative feelings involved in referral process, (iii) tackling separation anxiety in one or two sessions, (iv) handling the questions factually, and (v) preparing the client for new contact.

When referral is done for availing of some concrete or specialised services, the caseworker may, if required, also assume the role of an advocate or liaison worker (broker). The broker links the client with the needed services and helps in consummating the deal. This requires thorough knowledge of services available in the community and the procedures involved in securing them. Advocacy may be required when the agency does not offer its services to the client. The social caseworker tries to interpret the rules, looks for exceptions and precedents, and pleads for services to the client. While assuming either of these two roles, the caseworker must assess the risk and time involved, i.e., cost-benefit analysis for self as well as for the client. In this process, efforts can also be made to help the client to secure these services on his own with his social, administrative and political pressures. If this is possible, the caseworker can work only as an enabler. In all cases of referral, consent of the client is important to help him to use the available services for his problems.

Recording

Recording is an extremely important method to learn social work practice. In fact, the very purpose of fieldwork, the heart of social work training, is defeated without recording of the interactions during fieldwork. Recording helps in learning, as one, while recording, gets an opportunity to reflect back upon his interactions and locate the wrongs committed by him. It helps him to organise and interweave his information, observations, thinking and verbal interactions with the client in a meaningful whole. He, in this process, develops conceptual clarity, and absorbs the knowledge received from supervisors and literature. While recording his interactions, he starts appreciating his role better. Apart from this recording serves administrative and research purposes also. Anyone can work on these records to see how different approaches used are helpful to serve the clientele and what modifications are required in the approaches to achieve the desired results. Records serve teaching purposes also as they can be used to discuss methods, skills, techniques, etc., in practice. Records are also used to *evaluate* appropriateness of the process used and the work done. It provides an opportunity to offer constructive criticism to the student/worker to take care of his deficiencies, and improve his performance. Recording, by itself, provides an opportunity to the caseworker to develop insight into his own personality and social functioning leading to a desirable change in him or her.

Records can be written in different ways. The most effective way is the process recording. Other ways (types) of recording are narrative, role recording, summary recording and abstract. Narrative, process and role recording form a continuum. A beginner in social work should start with narrative recording. In *narrative recording* everything that has happened is recorded as it has happened. The attempts are to reproduce the situation. It consists of all the statements, observations and comments of the worker. It is narration of the happenings, a detailed account of the events which go in the narrative recording.

A recording that is of inestimable value to the learners of social work methods is *process recording*. Process is a continuing development involving many changes. It is a series of actions, changes or functions that bring about an end or result. Process recording tries to record these developments and actions. These developments are directly and meaningfully related to understanding of the person-in-situation and the intervention process. It is selective in its recording. Interactions, which have direct bearing or meaning for intervention, are recorded and the rest of the details of interactions are discarded. The focus is not on the development of the events as such but on the developments relevant to understanding of, and intervening in the persons psycho-social life. In process recording the process of helping is recorded which includes the relevant conversations, observations and reactions of the worker in the developmental sequence. It gives an idea to the supervisor if the therapist (caseworker) has used his knowledge of human behaviour and social situations, if his reactions to the client's verbal and non-verbal communications are appropriate, and if planning for future is consistent with the presenting situation.

Role recording, a refined version of process recording, is highly selective in its approach and focuses on the role of the worker in his interaction with the client. *Summary recording* tries to summarise the interactions with focus on main events. It avoids detail of any event. It is useful for keeping the records of the work carried out. This is used in the regular practice when the therapist is hard-pressed for time. Summary recording saves time and labour when process recording comparatively is very time-consuming. *Abstract*, a condensed form of summary recording, presents the basic idea or action taken.

Process Record: An Example

After supervisory conference I visited my agency LNJP Hospital. When I reached the ward, my client was sleeping alone in her bed. Her eyes were open when I reached her bed though she could not see me. The reason was that she appeared preoccupied. When I wished her, she got up and sat on the bed. I found a packet of *bidis* on her bed. I wanted to know the name of the smoker. For a while, she hesitated in giving answer but after sometime she told me that she was in the habit of smoking, specially when she was alone and had nothing to do. I questioned her, "Do you know how much harmful *bidi* is?" She told me that 'tambaku' (tobacco) was very useful for intestinal disease. I questioned her and tried to know the person who told her. She said that while she was in her village, her friends gave this information. I informed her about its adverse effects on health and tried to convince her that her information was wrong through questioning and commenting. At the end she agreed with me but her speaking tone and facial expression showed that she wants to stop the conversation about *bidi*. Since I saw that it was getting difficult for her to continue to talk on smoking, I shifted the topic and tried to know about her injured leg. She told me that there was improvement in it. I then asked her about her diet. She told me that she took milk without sugar but she could not eat *dal* and *roti* because of bitter taste she has in mouth. I asked her, "Do you want to become alright? She answered in the affirmative. I told her, "If you really want to be alright, take proper diet, otherwise there will be little effect of medicines." I informed her, "You are taking such a strong medicine and if you don't take proper food, after sometime you will become very weak and wouldn't be able to walk properly and would remain in the bed". I said this because she did not like to remain lying in the bed for the whole day. In response to my advice she repeated that she could not eat food because of bitter taste of her mouth. I asked her, "Please tell me if the medicines were to sweet taste". She answered, "No, it is of bitter taste". I asked her, "Why do you take it if it is bitter". She replied that she took it because of her disease. I commented her that she could take these food also as a medicine as they are equally important for her recovery. She could take food in bits. She nodded her head in affirmation. The interview ended with a promise to see her on the next day.

Records in fieldwork must fully bring out the points of treatment process—study and diagnosis. All the fieldwork records must contain worker's role and reactions, information about the person and his situation, use of principles, techniques and knowledge of human behaviour and the supervisory inputs. While recording the interactions, one may start with identifying informations, referral (if applicable), purpose of the interaction, transactional process, assessment of each transactional sessions followed by self-evaluation and future plan. *Assessment* involves deriving meaning from the facts, bringing out etiological factors, locating resources, etc., as discussed in the chapter on treatment processes. Self-evaluation involves a critical assessment of one's role as a trainee-therapist and of the new learnings in the situation. Self-evaluation helps in absorption of knowledge and development of skills. Recording is a strong instrument to reinforce and strengthen learning of the trainee/student.

Narrative Record: An Example

On the first day of my visit to the hospital I met Dr. Kumar, Medical Officer and told him my purpose. He allowed me to go with him on round of the hospital. First of all, he took me around the first floor which was a male ward. He examined various patients and enquired about their problems. On the way, he told me about the patients who could get our help. The doctor was accompanied by the ward boy and a staff nurse. He ordered the nurse to remove the plaster of some patients and told her about the problems from plasters. To some patients, he recommended dressing. So, the ward boy was arranging all these things side by side. The doctor examined each case and asked the reason of their illness from the new patients. He was asking questions in a lighter mood. So, the patients felt at ease with him. He also enquired about their general problems.

At the end of the round, I was asked to talk to Sri Satpal who was 35. He was sitting in his bed surrounded by many people. I introduced myself and told him my purpose and enquired about him. He was beaten by his enemies. He had a broken leg, a broken arm with swollen cheeks. So, he was plastered at the leg and arm. The cheek was bandaged. This was because of a quarrel between him and his neighbour over the route for water to fields. His neighbour did not allow him to route the irrigation water through his land.

Some of the co-villagers brought him from the field to the village and then from there to the hospital. He was accompanied by his brothers and friends at the time of interview. They all told me about the reason of their quarrel. I told him that he could report these things to the police. He told me that he has registered the report in the police station. The police visited the village but was taking no further step. They were annoyed over the police action because it did not take any step against their neighbours. I enquired if he was getting medicines and food etc. He was supplied food by his brothers. They also brought medicines for him. His cheek was swollen and his eyes seemed to be injured and red. The doctor on the round told the patient to get his eyes checked in the eye outdoor but they did not listen to him. Then, I told him to get his eye checked by the eye specialist on the ground floor and they agreed to take him there. I enquired about his other health problems. He told me that he felt pain in his back, so he could not sleep well in the night. I left him after promising to see him again to talk further about his problem.

7

Social Casework Processes: Study and Diagnosis

Social casework is an ongoing process of exploration (study), assessment (diagnosis), formulation of goals and treatment planning, intervention (treatment), evaluation and termination (disengagement). Fern Lowry (1936) described this process as similar in form to a rope woven of multiple strands. When one cuts the rope at any point, all the component strands are exposed. In the same way, examination of social casework at any point of time reveals fact-finding, assessment (diagnosis) and intervention (treatment) taking place concurrently. The first three of the processes, viz., fact-finding (study), assessment and planning for intervention, represent simply the empirical methods of a science applied to a human problem in a social work context. This method involves seeking and ordering informations and determining the nature and strength of the evidence which supports it. The caseworker then makes inferences based on the information, theoretical knowledge, and the experience of himself and others. Tentative hypotheses are formed, re-examined, accepted and revised, or eliminated in the light of further information. This is a *continuous* process which begins with the first encounter with the client (helpee), takes place in every interview, and extends over the entire contact. It is fundamental to the formulation of researchable questions in social casework.

Before study (exploration), as a process of social casework, is discussed, it is better to discuss Intake (engagement), an administrative procedure followed in some welfare and medical agencies.

Intake

As stated above, it is an administrative procedure, and not a process of social casework, to take in the person with problem, i.e., admit him or enrol him as a client of the agency. This starts with first encounter and ends with usually the second interview with the intake worker. This phase requires a very skilful probing into the client's problem, mopping up all the relevant areas of the person-in-his-situation.

During one or two skilfully conducted interviews with the would-be client, the caseworker (sometimes called as intake worker) is able to assess (i) what are the needs/problems of applicant person, and (ii) how and where his needs can be best met. This obviously requires that the caseworker finds out the nature of need, if it can be met in the present set-up of agency's policies, procedures, services and personnel, and what sort of competence and provisions will be helpful and is required to tackle his problems. How does the worker view the person and his problems diagnostically is also important to be mentioned. If his agency cannot serve the client's needs, which agency and which type of service are required to tackle his problems, and the need for referral are also decided at this stage by the intake worker (caseworker).

Areas for probing are: (i) the stage of the problem at which the person, through whom, and the reasons because of which, comes to this agency; (ii) the nature of request and its relation to his problem, and the cause of his problem, as the client sees; (iii) does the request relate directly to his needs/problems; (iv) his adjustment to his social functions in job, family, etc.; (v) the state of his physical and mental health; (vi) his appearance including dress etc. in the first meeting; (vii) his personal and social resources including material and financial position; (viii) appropriateness and intensity of feelings; (ix) nature of defense mechanisms he frequently uses; (x) level of motivation, i.e., how quickly he wants to get rid of his problems, the efforts he did in the past to solve it, sufferings because of the problem he had to face, and what efforts he is thinking to undertake to solve his problems; (xi) nature of family, its status, values, relationship pattern within the family etc.; and (xii) reactions to the worker and seeking help from the agency and sex of caseworker who will be suitable to help the person.

Thus, these questions will give a broad picture of the person, his physical and social environments, and the nature of their interaction which have given birth to these problems. No detailed probing is required; all that is required is to have a global appreciation of the person-in-his-situation to decide feasibility of his treatment in the agency and if required, to refer him to a suitable agency.

Techniques are the same as described earlier but the approach has to be that of a short-term, in which focusing is on relevant issues. Intake interviews are different from the initial interviews in casework process because intake does not aim at treating (helping) the case; at the best, it clarifies certain issues necessary to seek effective help. After intake, the case is usually referred to a particular caseworker or the intake caseworker himself/herself can continue with the case. Intake procedures are not followed in formal way in most of the welfare agencies. Only a few employ intake caseworkers. Usually, the caseworker, who is assigned the case, continues with the client or may dispose of by referring the client to some other expert or agency. Intake procedures, if implemented properly, help the agency to avoid wastage of its services, frustration to client, and in utilising its resources more effectively.

Psycho-social Study

According to Richmond (1917), the caseworker must secure all and every fact that taken together, through logical and inferential reasoning, would reveal the client's personality and his situation for appropriate intervention (treatment). An exhaustive collection of facts about the client and his situation is called study—the first step (process) in the continuum. (I will prefer to use the word 'study' because it communicates the real and complete nature of activities undertaken during this phase).

Psycho-social study is an ongoing process which begins with the first knowledge of the case, takes place in every interview, and extends over the entire contact. It may be defined as that part of the casework process which brings together the facts about a case and is distinctly different from the assessment of the meaning of the facts. Psycho-social study involves exploration, observation and documentation of both objective and subjective facts from a variety of sources.

In casework, the primary source of information is the client. One must learn when to go beyond personal report and seek data from collaterals, experts, significant others, documents (records), psychological tests, and so forth. One must be careful to carry out this search acting in full respect for the client, maintaining confidentiality, and without violating the right of the client to participate in, so far as it is possible.

Mutual engagement in the process is essential. It provides the caseworker with the client's own view of the problem. It gives the client an opportunity to clarify the problem in its various aspects, permits him to air his feelings about his situation, and gives him a satisfaction that genuine efforts are being made to help him.

While fact-gathering proceeds until the case is closed, there is usually an *emphasis* on study at the time a case is opened. The extent and breadth of this study depends on the situation presented by the client, the purpose and goals in seeking help, the situation as perceived by the worker, the range of treatment modes available, treatment potential and motivation for treatment, and on the agency structure and function. One needs to learn to determine the kind of study to be carried out in relation to these factors.

Investing of more time in study has been found to be frustrating to the client who seeks immediate help with the presenting problem. In any case, facts are needed to plan the intervention (treatment). While collecting data, one must see that it is relevant, salient and individualised. *Relevant* means facts "bearing upon or properly applying to the case in hand; of a nature to afford evidence tending to prove or disprove the matters in issue". It then implies that the way, in which the problem is presented and defined, treatment modalities and resources available etc. will determine which data are relevant and which part needs more exploration and observation. It follows then that study need not in every case cover each and every part of the person and situation. *Salient* implies prominence, i.e., anything which is conspicuous and noticeable. Similarly, *individualised* data mean that the data should be collected for a particular client having particular needs/ problems in a particular situation.

Facts required are either related to resources, structure of the organisation (system), e.g., family, agency, etc., communication, cultural practices, developmental stages, political situation, attitudes and behaviours of the client system, values and beliefs of individuals and groups, or to their multidimensional interaction with each other. These points have been elaborated in the section on assessment (diagnosis) to follow.

It must be emphasised that this conceptualisation of psycho-social study as a separate process is artificial and is used only to clarify and define the different types of activities involved in helping process. In practice, psycho-social study is carried out simultaneously with assessment and intervention. It is carried out through interview with the client, home visits, consultation of records and collateral contacts. It is different from *case history* or interviewing for research purposes. Interviews are conducted with emphasis on knowing the client, his situation and the nature of their interaction and not as question-answer session. Interviews are conducted in natural way with the help of interviewing techniques and the purpose in mind. It is the purpose which guides the interview.

To collect relevant data, one requires theoretical knowledge of human behaviour usually from the social and behavioural sciences.

Psycho-social Diagnosis (Assessment)

Gardener while discussing the therapeutic process from the point of view of psycho-analytic theory, says that "etiology, diagnosis and therapy are inseparably linked theoretically and practically in every approach to any of the disabilities of man". Since social casework services are addressed to free the man from his psycho-social and socio-psychological disabilities, diagnosis (assessment) is the inseparable part of helping process.

The process of diagnosis in social casework, according to Lowry (1936), consists of (1) shifting the relevant from irrelevant data, (2) organising the facts and getting them into relatedness, (3) grasping the way in which the facts fit together, and (4) perceiving the configuration of meaning as a whole. Assessment (diagnosis) of facts is done by the caseworker in the light of his theoretical orientation and knowledge, and the methods of intervention available to him. Diagnosis (assessment), psycho-social in nature, emphasises an understanding of psychological, biological, social and environmental factors operating on the 'person-in-his-situation'. This, in turn, affects the interview process and techniques used for further work with the client. This assessment gives a certain direction to the future work with the case.

Diagnosis may be viewed as a "fluid, constantly changing assessment of the client, their problems, life situations, and important relationships". As such diagnosis in social casework is an ongoing process.

According to Perlman (1957), diagnosis process involves examining the part of a problem for their particular nature and organisation, for the interrelationships among them, for the relation between them and the means to their solution. Thus, the diagnostic process, according to her, includes the conclusions this process leads to, stating what the trouble seems to be, how it is related to the goal, and what means the agency, caseworker and client himself can bring to bear upon the trouble. According to Perlman (1957), casework diagnosis consists of the (1) nature of the problem brought and the goals sought by the client in relationship to, (2) nature (personality) of the person who bears the problem, his social and psychological situation and functioning, and who seeks (or needs) help with his problem in relation to, and (3) nature and purpose of the agency and the kind of help it (agency) can offer and/or make available.

The diagnostic process, which is perceiving the situation in an organised way and deriving meaning from the available facts about the mentioned areas, starts at the first contact with the client and continues till termination of the casework services. The inferences or tentative conclusions derived from the facts in the light of theoretical knowledge (in other words, "what do the facts mean?") lead to and form the psycho-social diagnosis.

These inferences or hypotheses should be stated in terms of theoretical concepts, constructs and models that currently explain human behaviour and social processes. Thus, the psycho-social diagnosis is to state as specifically as possible the physical, emotional and social causes of the problem and the appropriate treatment plan for the person-in-his-situation. Diagnosis based on a few facts is hazardous. It is not a separate phase of the casework process, rather it goes *concurrently* with the study and intervention. No therapist can afford to wait for study and diagnosis to be completed before he takes up treatment.

Why Diagnosis

The client seeks help to solve his problems. To solve problems, one must know the causes. The diagnostic process helps in organising these causative factors in one whole, thereby making it more meaningful. One can see the whole and its parts in relation to each other. How various factors are related to each other and to the problem become very much visible. This gives a boundary and direction to the attempts of the helper in planning his helping process. This helps in (i) determining the focus of treatment, further collection of facts and discarding the irrelevant facts, and (ii) deciding the best course of action to solve the problem. Goals and techniques of treatment are accordingly decided on the basis of the diagnostic evaluation (assessment) of the facts.

Types of Diagnosis

The person-in-his-situation can be understood and described from dynamic, etiological and clinical angles. Diagnosis, then, may be classified into three types, viz., clinical, etiological and dynamic (Perlman, 1957).

In the *clinical diagnosis*, the person is described by the nature of his illness, e.g., schizophrenic, psychopath, typhoid, etc. This type of description implicitly includes "nature of the problem and its relation to the person and the helping means and goal". The clinical diagnosis is the subject of medical practice. Its use in casework practice is minimum and no attempt is made in social casework to undertake clinical diagnosis as it is of little value in planning casework intervention (treatment). However, the social workers working with medical and psychiatric patients need a fairly good understanding of various implications of clinical diagnosis (medical terms) useful while working in collaboration with medical and para-medical experts. In the recent past, psychiatric social workers in India have been encouraged to develop a capacity to diagnose patients clinically (though broadly only) because of the fact that they have to work very closely with psychiatrists in the treatment of the psychiatric patients (Nayyar, 1965).

The *etiological diagnosis* tries to delineate the causes and development of the presenting difficulty which may lie in the life situation or/and in the client's personality. The present problem is seen in terms of past events and experiences. This is important to understand because it gives an idea of the duration, consistency and strength of the problem in the life history of the client or patient. It also tells how far a particular disturbance has been affecting his social functioning, why his particular inappropriate behaviour has been persisting, how he has been coping with the problems, what are his personal strengths and how far these causative factors can be modified or altered.

However, etiological diagnosis has its own limitations. There are problems of current adjustment of individuals which cannot be explained fully on the basis of analysis of the life history of the person or problem. Its limitation has been very appropriately put in by Richmond (1922) when she quotes Jung: "A person is only half understood when one knows how everything in him came about. Only a dead man can be explained in terms of the past." Hence dynamic diagnosis should be concurrently undertaken to supplement the understanding of the man as he is today.

Dynamic diagnosis seeks a proper evaluation of the client's current problem as he is experiencing it now. It seeks to identify the various factors in active play in the current person-situation configuration. It is a cross-sectional view of the forces currently operating in the client's problem. The dynamic diagnosis seeks to establish what the trouble is, what role psychological, biological, social and environmental factors are playing in the causation of the problems, what effect it (the problem) has on the individual's well-being (and that of others related with the client), what solution is sought, and what means exist within the client, his situation and the organised services and resources by which the problem may be affected. In dynamic diagnosis, there is no attempt to dig the life history of the problem, rather reasons for the problem are traced in the current situation. Thus dynamic approach focuses on the forces (instinctual needs) and their satisfaction, interaction of thinking and emotions and between the structural parts (id, ego, etc.) of personality which are currently operating within the client, and on interaction between him and his social and physical situations.

In sum, diagnosis (assessment) includes "interpretation of the facts, evaluation of the several value systems, and the comparison of the validity and feasibility of various solutions and its results in operational predictions". The diagnosis, a tentative conclusion subject to modification, is a continuing process, and as such a dynamic activity. The following outlines may prove quite useful for study and diagnostic purposes.

A Format for Psycho-social Study and Diagnosis

Identifying Information

Place clients in their current social reality, i.e., according to age, sex, race, religion, nationality, marital status, ordinal position in the family, and socio-economic class, occupation, current living situation, i.e., housing, other members in family etc. Observe affect, clothing, grooming, speech, gait, posture, muscular tension, facial expression, vasomotor responses in presence of, and interaction with, others. Changes in behaviour; reaction to social worker, etc.

Presenting Problem

This includes problem for which client seeks help including source of and reason for referral, whether problem is of recent origin or of long standing, what precipitated client to seek help, client's reaction to problem, his reacting to the referral source, and to the agency and worker as sources of help. It also includes what has been done about the problem. Significance of the problem to the client and significant others and how disturbing the problem is to them. Past therapeutic experience. Client's expectations of help.

Assessment of Current Social Functioning and Immediate Social Situations

(a) 1. *Family relationships*: What is family's style of functioning, goals, values, power structure, communication patterns, role patterns, joint and nuclear family arrangements, etc.

2. *Interpersonal relationships*: What is occurring with significant others at work and recreation; nature of communication patterns, his reference groups, etc.

3. Adequacy of role performances in family, work and other situations.

(b). *Personality structure and dynamics of functioning*:

1. The efficiency of ego structure to deal with current inner forces, the current reality situations, and the interplay of both. Capacity of the client to observe self.

2. The nature and appropriateness of ego mechanisms in relation to social factors and influences of current exterior pressures. Indications of capacity to make modifications or the necessity of maintaining and strengthening existing defenses.
   - Prominent ego defenses (e.g., repression, denial, etc.).
   - Super-ego (strength, rigidity and integration).
   - Adaptive strengths (e.g., adequacy of reality testing, degree of synthesis within the ego, stress tolerance, amount of energy available for adaptive tasks).

3. Sense of self (e.g., body image, control vs. being influenced, etc.).

4. Psycho-social modalities (e.g., trust vs. mistrust, identity vs. role diffusion, etc.).
5. Prominent affects (e.g., depression, guilt, anxiety, hospitality etc.).
6. Nature and degree of problem (an etiological diagnosis and/or dynamic diagnosis should be used).

(c) Intellectual endowment (intellectual capacity).

(d) *Health of client*: Observe and see the medical reports if available.

History

Assessment of the nature of the client's problem in the light of history. Tie together the significant factors in cause-effect relationship as seen from history.

Includes psycho-dynamic, somatic and socio-cultural factors. If history does not contain sufficient information about a specific aspect, it is well to indicate that this is unclear, thus pointing up areas for further exploration and assessment.

A Brief Diagnostic Summary Statement

Restate all relevant facts and inferences including clinical diagnosis. State the relative seriousness of each aspect and of all the possible causes and aspects in relation to each other. Also state *prognosis*. Assess the client's motivation and capacity to use help. Specify short and long range goals. Include the kind and amount of change to be expected. State all appropriate services needed. Specify casework techniques for accomplishing the goals. Also specify environmental factors which may help or hinder casework and any other recommended services. Are recommended services available in the community?

Diagnosis, Goals and Intervention Plan Need to be Re-evaluated in the Light of New Facts

As a professional member of the agency staff, we should consider the following also:

(a) Nature, severity and frequency of problem:
- which groups are most likely affected by the problem,
- observe shifts or changes in relation to problem.

(b) Evaluation of treatment facilities related to problem:
- appropriateness of agency services in light of the problem,
- availability of, or gaps, in community resources in relation to problem,
- what broad social planning would prevent or mitigate development of such a problem?

(c) What is the appropriate channel for action at necessary level?
- agency,
- community,
- broad social planning.

Causative factors may also be identified and evaluated along several other dimensions. They may be:

1. *Lack of resources*: Sometimes lack of resources may cause or contribute to the development of the problem. Resources may be either financial, educational, health, recreational or housing etc.
2. *Structural*: It is the very form of the system (organisation) working as a factor in causation or precipitation of the problem? (This includes the internal organisation of individuals, families, agencies and other relevant systems, and communities). For example:
   - the single-parent family;
   - a very small house for a very large family;
   - a lack of understanding regarding who makes decisions;
   - too much concentration of power in one person or sub-system;
   - imbalance in the membership of a small group, or committee, or city council etc. Is the system an open or closed one?

3. *Communication*: Is there dysfunctional (ineffective or contradictory or hostile) communication pattern? What can be the reasons for this?
4. *Cultural*: Are there marked cultural or sub-cultural differences within the system (family or other units) or between the relevant systems. How do these contribute to the problem? What bearing do these have on communication patterns, decisions making, and on attitudes and behaviours of the client.
5. *Development*: What is the relationship of the stage of development of the particular client (system) to the nature of the problem? How does it relate, for instance, to family structure and communication patterns? To what extent does the newness or the long existence of an organisation have a bearing on the flexibility or rigidity of the organisation? How do the significant events in the system's past influence its current functioning?
6. *Political*: To what extent do political forces have a bearing on the problem? To what extent do such factors as use of power, power struggles, competition, ability to tolerate and resolve conflict, needs to gain more power or to bring about changes in the location of power, etc., have a bearing on the problem?
7. *Attitudes and behaviour*: To what extent are emotions and behaviours (per se, or in relation to the problem with which the client is struggling) dysfunctional (inappropriate or inadequate)? What is the system's previous problem-solving history? For example, resourcefulness vs. hopelessness, resoluteness vs. indecision, concern vs. apathy, constructive action vs. protection of the status quo, etc. Are there internal forces (within personality) which tap the available energies for problem-solving? Are there external environmental stresses which impair the system's problem-solving capacities?
8. *Values and beliefs*: Are the problems related to different values and beliefs held by various individuals or sub-systems

(components) of the system, and between the system and its environment? What are the influences, here, of cultural and sub-cultural background, and life aspirations? What is the history and what are the traditions? To what extent do these aspects have a bearing on the problem? How is the value and belief system of the social worker perceived by the client system and to what extent does this affect problem-solving efforts?

Social caseworker should use these guidelines for collection of data and prepare diagnosis based on the interpretation of the facts collected.

Intervention Plan and Goal Setting

The purpose, for which social study and psycho-social assessment (diagnosis) are undertaken, is casework intervention (treatment). The first stage in intervention (treatment) involves planning. The questions to be answered by the worker at this stage are: "What kind of help (treatment) will best stabilise or improve the client's functioning or better meet his needs?" "In terms of the kind of social adaptation or adjustment, which will be of most value to him?" It is important to stress, however that each step in treatment must be taken jointly with the client since he is the person who will ultimately determine his engagement in this process. The aptitude, skills and knowledge of the individual worker may promote the treatment (helping) process or impede it. It is also important to re-emphasise that the treatment plans are always conditioned by the age, health, culture, mores, values, opportunities, agency policy and community as well as broad societal forces. In addition, the caseworker has to be aware of his own norms and values and needs so that they are used constructively and do not interfere with the helping (treatment) process.

Long-range Objectives

Treatment plans are clearly related to certain objectives. Among these are the following:

1. to restore or improve social functioning and increase capacity for self-direction;
2. to prevent deterioration and conserve strength; and
3. to create opportunities for growth and development.

In summation, the long-range objectives are to make people's life experiences more comfortable, compensating, satisfactory, productive and self-fulfilling.

Immediate Objectives

Goals are not static. They are in a process of becoming. Some of the first steps taken to help a case may determine or even become initial or final goals. For example, in the case of an aged helpless person, securing old age pension may be the initial as well as final goal. Objectives are related to and emanate from every aspect of a case situation with which one deals. Goals can alternatively become prominent or receding. Both long-range and immediate objectives relate to and are an outgrowth of the dynamic understanding of the case. One should plan his intervention in each case in terms of the considered immediate (short-term) objectives (prioritywise) in the determination of which the client participates. In fact, these short-term (immediate) objectives lead to achieve the long-term objectives. The objectives initially undertaken should meet his needs quickly and be reassuring to him. Once the objectives are set, the specific methods, techniques, type of services required and the expected improvement and change is also to be calculated tentatively.

These objectives, needless to say, are based on realistic and sound assessment of the client's social situation, needs and his priorities, motivations, capacities and resources available. Agency settings, modifiability of causative factors, time factor and caseworker's competence, etc., also impose certain limitations on choosing the objectives. Objectives set should be specific, realistic and achievable within the time limit.

Once this planning is complete, one can move with the case to achieve the desired objectives. This planning should be a continuous process and not a periodical one. In some cases, in India, discussing the planning with the client may not be feasible either for time factor or overall socio-educational level of the client. In such cases, planning (how the problem will be solved) should at least be shared with him. This may not be useful if it involves telling the client the process of therapy, i.e., what will be done and how it will solve his problems. Telling this to the client may weaken his motivation to seek help. This, to my experience, is quite true of majority of the Indian clients who do not, by and large, appreciate the invisible therapeutic process.

Intervention (treatment/execution/action) is the fourth step in the social casework process after study (fact-finding), diagnosis (assessment) and planning for action, which aims at restoring, maintaining or enhancing social functioning of an individual in need of help. All casework help intends (i) to improve the client's psycho-social functioning and bring positive changes in his adaptive patterns, and/or (ii) to improve environmental conditions and resources, and to make them available to the client for his growth and development. Implied in these goals are prevention of deterioration in and conserving the strength of the client.

The *approach* to treatment, then, can be said to include either or any combination of the following services:

(a) the administration of concrete and practical services;
(b) modification of environment, both social and physical;
(c) strengthening capacities or clarifying, modifying and reinforcing attitudes, beliefs and values favourable to change and growth or to maintenance of the emotional equilibrium.

To achieve the desired goals, many practice theories (i.e., how and what to do in given situation to achieve the specified changes) are available in social casework literature. A few of them currently more in use, will be taken up for elaboration in the next chapter. All these practice theories claim to deal with all the problems of psycho-social functioning. Finally, it remains up to the practitioner to decide the approach (based on a specific practice theory) of choice in every case. This decision of the practitioner will be partly dependent upon (1) the unit of consideration: individual, couple, family; (2) length of treatment: long-term, short-term, referral, transfer; (3) nature of situation: crisis or non-crisis; and (4) the nature of problem: interpersonal or economic, etc.

Intervention starts from the first contact with the client who seeks to solve his problems with the help of a social caseworker. In the *initial* phase, attempts are made to establish rapport and sustain the client's interest in solving his problems. Approach to intervention as described by Hollis (1972) is discussed below. The author has chosen this approach because it describes the process in toto and encompasses the usual problems dealt with by the caseworkers. Interviewing skills and techniques are used to achieve the goals. Principles constantly guide the activities of the caseworker. Privacy is important for conducting casework interviews. Knowledge of human behaviour helps in focusing on relevant aspects of behaviour. In another words, case work is carried out through interviewing (talking) techniques which help in achieving sub-goals (like perceiving the reality, developing understanding of the situation, insight into one's a particular behaviour, locating resources, improving relationship with someone, etc.). While doing so, worker remembers values and assumptions and is guided by principles and knowledge of human behaviour. Hollis describes the processes in her approach (see Chapter 8) as given below.

Sustaining Process (Initial Contact)

We all have experienced anxiety whensoever we had to ask for help from persons unknown or formally known to us. Similarly, questions about self from unknown or formally known persons also create anxiety in us. Apart from this, when the client approaches the caseworkers, he is naturally suffering from some anxiety caused by his problem/non-fulfilment of his needs. The anxiety is tackled and the client's interest in solving his problem is sustained. Sustaining process becomes more useful when anxiety is greater as it quickly reduces his anxiety, makes him comfortable and thus builds his confidence in caseworker.

Techniques used in sustaining process to maintain his/her current social functioning and interest in casework treatment are conveying acceptance, reassurance and encouragement. *Acceptance* is an attitude of warm goodwill towards the client, whether or not the client's behaviour is socially acceptable and whether or not he is liked by the caseworker. Conveying acceptance does not refrain the worker from communicating his evaluation of the client's social functioning to him but the only condition is that it should be done out of goodwill. Sustaining process is useful when the client feels guilty having come to seek help from the agency, or when, for some reasons, he feels unworthy of the worker's liking or respect. The worker continues to convey a positive and understanding attitude towards the client. This attitude is not dependent upon the nature of action or behaviour of the client. It is a continued expression of goodwill or positive concern towards the client. The worker extends the required respect, listens to him interestingly and communicates to the client (through his facial expression, tone of voice, choice of words and body postures) that he likes the client. The verbal and non-verbal communication of the worker should not be incongruent and contradictory. It should rather be supplementary to communicate acceptance. Acceptance can be communicated better only when the local norms and traditions for communicating respect are fully understood by the worker. Communication of acceptance is further facilitated by the worker's understanding of client's personal differences with the values of the group he belongs to, and the caseworker's own values. Awareness of one's feeling to punish or seek return in lieu of services being given, moralistic attitude, etc., will help in exhibiting the deep concern for the client. The real method to express acceptance is to work hard for solution of the client's problem.

The technique of *reassurance* brings relief to the client suffering from anxiety and guilt. Relief does not come from understanding but because the caseworker, in whom the client has placed confidence, has said in effect that it is not necessary to be so worried (see chapter on 'Interviewing' for reassurance and encouragement, the techniques used in sustaining process). Sustaining process may require use of gift, patting and fondling when working with children. Home visits or solving the pressing concrete piece of problem, etc., will sustain the client's interest in casework treatment and prevent further deterioration in his/her social functioning.

The process of *direct influence* deals with the different ways the worker uses to promote a specific kind of behaviour on the part of the client, i.e., he directly tries to bring a change in the client's behaviour usually in the situation demanding specific behaviour like how to handle the child, how to deal with the employer, etc. This is achieved because of the client's trust in the worker. The trust of the client in the worker is used as a vehicle for influencing his behaviour. Hollis (1972) classifies the areas where direct influence is more useful:

1. Child-rearing matters.
2. Anxious people till they do not develop self-confidence.
3. Infantile personality.
4. Persons whose sense of reality is weak.
5. Compulsive patients.

The technique of direct influence should be used only when the worker knows that a particular (the suggested) course of action will be more useful and is perhaps the best in the situation for the client. This process should be used only when the client *really* needs it, i.e., when the situation of the client justifies use of this process. Many a time this process is used just because the workers in our settings are more anxious to give suggestions/advice, and sometimes, the client may ask for suggestions/advice only to please the worker.

According to Hollis (1972) the techniques of direct influence are:

1. *Underlining*: This involves approving or emphasising a course of action, the client himself is contemplating upon. Here, the worker may use the sentences like, "I think this is realistic for you to...", "I think you are doing the right thing and the action should be taken as quickly as possible".
2. *Suggestion*: Herein a solution is raised in the client's mind by the worker and it is up to the client to accept or reject the idea. Since the worker is not emphatic on this suggestion, the client is free to reject the idea. For example, worker may say, "You can utilise this leisure time for painting or kitchen-garden etc." In case the client uses his leisure time for walking or playing, he is free to do so without any fear of criticism from the worker.
3. *Advice*: This involves stating an opinion or taking a stand concerning certain issues which must be acted upon by the client in his own interest and which if not taken will be harmful to the client's interest. Physicians advise drugs which should be taken by the client if he wants to get cured. He does not suggest a drug when the patient is sick rather he advises. Similarly, the caseworker advises actions which should be adopted by the client to solve the problems.
4. *Advocating*: This is one step beyond the advice, i.e., putting a certain urgency behind the advice offered. Advice is re-emphasised. It is offered in term of "it is essential and that it would be very unwise not to do so". This is indicated when there is a chance of severe loss because of the client's

ill-considered or impulsive action or when enough time is not available for discussing consequences of the action being contemplated by the client. Such situations may be like a mentally disturbed person sticking to the home, a person likely to commit suicide, or running away from home, etc. In all such situations, advocating becomes more useful because it saves the client from the big loss he may suffer because of his ill-considered action. However, no attempt should be made to create guilt in the client, when he fails, by telling him that "I told you so".

5. *Actual intervention*: Herein the caseworker takes action to prevent the client from taking inadequately considered action or sees that he acts in a particular (the desirable) way. Examples are removing the patient to a hospital, placing the child in a hostel, etc. Use of this technique demands that the worker be fully convinced that the step is factually justified and necessary community resources and support are available. His action should be firm and polite without communicating any anxiety to the people around.

Direct influence techniques should be avoided unless it is really justified and it should be, wherever possible, used in conjunction with the procedures for development of understanding. To start with, most gentle form of influence should be used. The caseworker has to be very cautious and conscious of his own needs while suggesting and offering advice.

Ventilation Process

The process of ventilation (catharsis) is the process of helping the client to air his feelings freely and to provide him with an atmosphere which makes free expression of the feelings easier. It frees the individual from fears, guilt feelings, and brings to light the hidden attitudes. The more intense the feelings, the better result through this process. This is usually used when the client is more tense or eager to come out with his inner feelings.

This technique may be used in certain unpleasant situations which might have arisen in between the interviews. Ventilation is not only therapeutic but also diagnostic. The therapist should explore intently and stimulate the client, by questioning or commenting, to tell more about his situation and its various aspects. Only towards the end of session, the caseworker may use generalisation and logical discussion to lessen his guilt. In the initial stages one should not minimise the anxiety lest he stops coming out with relevant materials necessary to help him. The caseworker may choose either to be totally passive or actively participating and directing. The client must feel that the worker is uncritical, tolerant and is listening to him.

One should not permit ventilation when it is used as a defense mechanism to avoid further exploration. In such situations, it is better to divert his attention and help him to discuss the relevant matters concerning his problem. It should be avoided or used with caution in case of psychotics etc. Ventilation is used sometimes by the client to seek attention and sympathy from the worker or a gratification from talking freely about self. The caseworker should be conscious in all such situations and direct the interviews accordingly.

Reflective Discussion of the Current Person-Situation Configuration

As stated earlier, the psycho-social therapy views man in his situation and tries to understand the total man, i.e., inseparable from his environment. The procedure for reflective discussion, according to Hollis (1972), does not involve use of clarification or interpretation (utilised for developing insight). She has classified the procedure for discussion of current person-situation configuration into four sub-categories: (i) perception and knowledge, (ii) decisions and consequences (reactions), (iii) inner awareness, responses and distortions, and (iv) reactions to the worker and treatment. These are described in the paragraphs that follow.

Perception and Knowledge

In this category, caseworker is concerned with his/her client's current situation which may consist of people, events and conditions related to economic, social, physical and educational spheres of life. The procedure in this sub-category deals partly with perception and partly with the question of knowledge.

Some of the clients see either distorted or only one-sided picture of the real situation around them. This happens because the clients see/hear what they anticipate or because their intense feeling lead them to ignore certain aspects of the real situation. The feelings may also blot out important aspects of the reality. The worker may, in such situations, draws the attention of the client to the real facts of the situation which may in many cases correct his distorted perception of the situation. If this procedure does not work, the client may be helped to perceive the discrepancies between reality and his views of it, without going into the dynamics of his perceiving reality into a distorted way.

When we are angry with our friend or relative, we see his negative points only and interpret his good behaviour also from a negative angle only. His help is interpreted as motivated by selfish ends etc. In such cases, every movement of the friend/relative is interpreted in the same light and the reality gets totally ignored or blurred.

An individual's response to a person may, sometimes, be because of little knowledge the individual has about normal responses of the concerned categories of persons like adolescents/aged/children etc. Explanations and informations may develop understanding in the client leading him to tolerate normal reactions of the people. When an adolescent reacts angrily to the parents' sermons for work/good behaviour, they should be helped to understand and appreciate the characteristic ways of behaviour of this age group.

In some situations the client may be hostile to others just because he is unable to imagine their feelings in the situation, or because of his failure to identify with the feelings of the person. A husband may not appreciate the difficulties of a university educated housewife, unable to manage household affairs effectively, simply because he fails to imagine the possible responses and feelings of such a housewife in such a situation. Similarly, a wife failing to appreciate the tiredness of her husband after he returns home from his work, may start murmuring the moment he enters the house.

Understanding of the external world can be increased if help (guidance) is extended in respect of various important life events like family budget, work situation, physical conditions, involvement in some social situation etc. If proper guidance is extended in these matters, e.g., how to prepare family budget, whom to approach for this or that work etc., the client will be able to handle his situation more effectively conducive to his growth and development.

Techniques like logical discussion, questioning, etc., which lead the client to think through is found to be more convincing and lasting in its affects. Explanation may not be very effective. Informing or use of bibliography can also be tried alongwith other techniques in helping the client to reflect upon various aspects of his current situation.

Decisions and Consequences (Reactions)

In this procedure we consider the decisions and activities of the client and its effects in interaction with his environment. Over and again the worker strives to help the client think about the effect of his decisions and actions on others or its consequences for himself, e.g., advantages and disadvantages of moving to a new job, place, seeking divorce, quarreling with boss, and purchasing properties etc. In any of these instances, the client tries imaginatively with the help of the caseworker to foresee the consequence of the plan for himself and for the other people whose lives are involved in his decision. The worker brings the client's attention to those aspects of the situation which he may have overlooked, and this helps in right decisions. The decision should be taken after all possible facts have been gathered and the pros and cons of the alternative decisions have been considered.

At other times, an understanding of the effects of the client's own behaviour or someone else involved in the situation is the focus of discussion. To quote Hollis (1972), a mother may not realise that hitting her son compels him to defy her to maintain his prestige before his peers. If possible, avoid explaining the relationship between behaviour and consequences. It is preferable to lead the client to see sequence himself. Many times the client will draw his own correct conclusion once the two aspects of his behaviour are brought to his attention.

Inner Awareness, Responses and Distortions

This part involves awareness of the so-called hidden feelings or reactions. There are many degree of hiddenness, according to Hollis (1972). The client may be perfectly aware of his reactions but afraid to speak of it because he is ashamed of it or fears ridicule or criticism, or has not recognised the significance of his feeling. At times, the client may be truly unaware of his feelings because they are not part of his conscious thoughts.

There are occasions when reading his thoughts is necessary, either because the client, unable to bring out his thoughts into open will feel relieved if the worker does so for him, or, because there is therapeutic justification for bringing them out even though this may make him uncomfortable. Skill lies in finding ways of enabling the client to bring out the hidden material himself. Where full awareness is present, this often occurs without any specific prompting as the client becomes more secure with the worker in response to a sustaining approach. If, however, the client is struggling with the question of whether to speak something or not, the caseworker may handle this hesitation directly by commenting, "I understanding you want to talk about your relationship with". At other times, when the worker is fairly sure of what the client is withholding, he may be able to make comments which refers tangentially to the anticipated content, thus inviting the client to talk about it but still not facing him with it directly, e.g., "You want to say that you want to leave the school".

Often one can use the procedure of calling the attention of the client to the discrepancies between facts and feelings, to overemphasis, or to inconsistencies or inappropriateness one sees in the feelings. Sometimes this can be done merely by repeating the revealing statement in a questioning tone. For example, one can say, "You don't like to meet your wife?"

When it is actually advisable to put the matter into words for the client, this can be done tentatively, making it possible for the client to maintain his defenses if he needs to do so. This also safeguards him from agreeing too readily to a possibly incorrect interpretations when the worker is not certain of his perception of the helpee's thinking. Occasionally, a direct unqualified interpretation is helpful, but for this the worker should be very sure of his ground.

When the client's attention is called to irrational or unproductive behaviour, he may on his own consider the consequences of his behaviour or the reasons for it, according to Hollis (1972).

When feelings are brought to expression, the worker can adopt any of the technique---sustaining, discussion of genetic and dynamic matter or client's current situations.

Reactions to the Worker and Treatment

The client's negative reactions to the worker's performance, the treatment process, or to agency rules and regulations may block improvement in the client and may ultimately wean the client away from the agency and worker. This may happen when the nature of the casework process, expected outcome, worker's role and agency's policies and regulation are not covered in the initial discussions between them. This may happen also because of transference and distorted perception of the process and of the worker's efforts etc.

Techniques used in this procedure are demonstrating realities of interaction between client and caseworker and of his behaviour towards him, explaining the reasons for his certain behaviour giving knowledge and information, recognising and discussing the hurdles in the treatment, spacing the interview, exploring certain attitudes, accepting one's feelings and reactions, etc.

Procedure for Reflective Consideration of Patterns of Personality and Behaviour, and their Dynamics

This procedure is designed for those persons who cannot benefit adequately from the earlier procedure because of intrapsychic forces operating behind their patterns (tendencies) of behaviour. Consideration of patterns of personality and behaviour does not involve probing early life experiences. It seeks "to pursue intrapsychic reasons" for the feelings, attitudes, ways of acting and thus the specific interaction between emotions and thoughts causing problems to the client. How the libidinal (sex urges) and aggressive drives are seeking satisfaction? Is their satisfaction creating anxiety in client?

In cases where the client is vaguely aware of his unrealistic or inappropriate behaviour, the caseworker may point out and draw his attention to it. If required, reality may be demonstrated alongwith discussion of the feelings and thoughts involved in the said inappropriate behaviour. Many a time, the client does not understand/realise that his behaviour is not conducive to his proper social functioning (i.e., it is ego-dystonic or ego-alien behaviour) and that he should change his pattern of behaviour so that it really becomes ego-syntonic, i.e., conducive to his development. A student who coerces his classmates to leave the class is indulging in ego-dystonic behaviour though he thinks it to be ego-systonic. To help such students (clients) one has to first help him to realise that his behaviour is, in fact, ego-dystonic, therefore, non-congenial to his proper social functioning.

Unconscious matters revealed through dreams etc., are utilised though no attempt is made to uncover this part of the mind. Too much of use of defense mechanisms speaks of poor capacity of ego to tolerate frustrations and consequent anxiety. In such cases, one may first bring these instances to his notice and slowly interpret it in dynamic terms, i.e., how and why he used it frequently or inappropriately.

Similarly, he may be helped to recognise his impulsive behaviour to learn to control such behaviours. Certain clients suffer from excessive guilt because of too strong superego. In such cases too one may first bring the facts to his notice (i.e., recognise it) and then, if required, may discuss its inappropriateness with reference to the social reality.

When the personality needs of dependence, narcissism, self-importance become excessive, these cause problems and hinder the client's normal social functioning. Similarly, his unrealistic beliefs about caste, religion, etc., may also distort his perception and lead him to behave in socially unacceptable or undesirable way apart from inviting troubles from various quarters. All these get reflected in the client's interaction with the caseworker or his description of current social interactions.

Insight into the current dynamics (interplay and interaction) of his feelings, responses, behaviour in his current interaction with others leads him to improvement. To develop insight one should try to understand the emotional process, their origin (may be dissatisfaction of drives) and defense mechanisms used. *Techniques* may be clarification and interpretation, confrontation and logical discussion etc.

An attempt is also made in this procedure to understand how a behaviour is continuing to exist inspite of its being counter-productive. Reinforcing factors behind these counter-productive behaviours have to be located and tackled.

Positive reinforcement is required to strengthen the newly learnt behaviour.

Procedures of Reflective Consideration of the Past Development and its Effect on Current Function

This procedure considers the genetic material (early childhood experiences) operating in the client's current behaviour patterns (response tendencies). Hollis (1972) pleads for use of this procedure only when the earlier procedures fail to yield desirable results (i.e., the desired change in the behaviour pattern of the client).

In certain cases, improvement in the desired direction does not occur because of deep influence of the client's earlier life experiences in his current functioning. These influences block his efforts to change in the required direction. Therefore, it becomes imperative to help the client to see the links between his present personality characteristics and earlier life experiences. Once the client is able to perceive how his earlier life experiences have shaped his certain current behaviour patterns (tendencies), he can be helped to review his earlier life experiences (if it can be recalled properly) and modify his reactions to these earlier experiences. These "dysfunctional characteristics (or tendencies to behave in a particular style) cannot be overcome unless he develops insight into how these experiences have shaped his present dysfunctional behaviour patterns or tendencies. This is based on Freudian concepts, according to which childhood experiences have permanent effect on personality functioning. However, it has been now realised that earlier life experiences get modified and the later experiences are as much valuable as the earlier ones.

This procedure does not seek to understand all the determinants of a particular behaviour pattern simply because it is not possible according to modern behavioural sciences and as implied in Indian philosophical concept of 'anekantwad'. In this procedure also, positive reinforcers for a particular behaviour pattern are to be located and handled.

Earlier misconceptions or distorted generalisations get confirmed or reinforced by later experiences. To quote an example, a girl aged 20 years was unwilling to marry a college teacher because according to her, teachers have poor social life and status. On enquiry, it was revealed by her that this was based on her experience of her father. Her distorted generalisation got reinforced from her experiences of her neighbours also. It may be mentioned that in such cases, clients perceive what they want to perceive and recognise only those experiences which confirm their ideas (misconceptions or distorted generalisations as discussed earlier with reference to current person-situation configuration). As opined earlier, no attempt is made to uncover the unconscious or retrace the infantile experiences, except those which can be easily recalled with normal probing. No technique of psycho-analysis to understand unconscious is used.

According to Hollis (1972), the client may talk about the past (1) for explaining his problem/disease, (2) for ventilating his feelings and pressure, (3) to justify his present feelings, attitudes and behaviour, and (4) because he thinks that the worker is interested in the history of the past. The caseworker may draw the attention of the client to the inconsistencies in his behaviour or examine his past experiences in the light of realities prevailing then.

In the case of a mother who does not allow her university educated girls for marketing, the caseworker can help to link her this behaviour with her own experience of moving along when unmarried. Sometimes this behaviour of mother may be because she learnt from her parents to restrict the movement of unmarried girls. In such a case, the link between her present behaviour and her experience of parental restriction can be established and examined and re-evaluated (in terms of the realities existing then) to develop insight. However, re-evaluation of the past experiences should be taken up only when recognition of the past's influence on current functioning fails to bring change in the client's social functioning.

The phenomenon of transference occurring in the transactions between the caseworker and client may also be used to understand the past's (i.e., genetic) influence in the current functioning of the client. To quote an example, the caseworker may comment, "You want me to accompany you to Red Cross as your father used to do". Here, the client's dependence that he had developed on father is reflected in the relationship with caseworker and the client is thus transferring his experience with father onto the present interaction with the caseworker as he unconsciously identifies the caseworker with father (authority) figure.

It may be mentioned that before attempting dynamic or genetic (developmental) understanding, the caseworkers should use sustaining process and ventilation. Interpretations should always be in tentative terms unless one is dead sure of the meaning of the behaviour. Dependence of the client on caseworker for self-understanding should be minimised and he should be encouraged to think more on himself. It is always better to lead the client to think on his own than giving him readymade answers or solutions, in other words, caseworker should work *with* the client and not *for* the client.

Under the *indirect* casework, the caseworker works with people other than the client because these people can be helpful to the improvement in the client's social functioning. One may work, in the case of an industrial worker, with the immediate supervisor, labour officer, wife, etc. In the case of a school-going child, one may work with the parents and teachers. The work with these people should be taken up only when one is satisfied that these people are affecting the client's functioning and can be helpful to effect change in his social functioning. Apart from working with significant others, one may arrange for concrete services like admission to a hospital, widow or old age pension, money for purchase of some equipments/medicines, etc. While arranging these *protective* services, the caseworker should assess if these services will be helpful to his social functioning, i.e., these should be used as a tool to help him to perform satisfactorily in his various roles. While serving the client, the caseworker can work in the role of a provider, locator, creator, interpreter, mediator and aggressive intervener (Hollis, 1972).

Thus, Hollis' classification is broad enough to tackle and handle most of the problems one faces in social work settings. Concepts drawn from various other approaches can be used alongwith this approach. These approaches can be used as supplementary to each other. While working with rural population and tradition-bound families, use of Indian concepts has been found quite useful.

Evaluation

In recent years evaluation has assumed a significant place in our service programmes. It has been realised that no service or project can be effective unless we continuously and intermittently evaluate the outcomes of programmes and effectiveness of the methods used to deliver services. A lot of literature has, in the last decade, emerged on evaluation of welfare services.

In social casework practice too, we need to evaluate, at least empirically, the outcome of our efforts. The purpose of evaluation, as a process of casework, is to see if our efforts are yielding any result or not, if the techniques used are serving the purpose, and if the goals are being achieved. This is not done from research point of view, because of which we do not use any rating scale etc. Like assessment (diagnosis), this too is a continuous process. Intermittently, evaluation of the approach and result should be taken up with the client so that the efforts are meaningfully utilised. These evaluations may tell if the problem needs redefinition, if the objectives are to be reassessed and redetermined, and if the intervention approach and techniques need any change. This will further strengthen the relationship between the helper and helpees and motivate the client to work towards his goal.

At the end, i.e., termination (see chapter on 'Interviewing'), the worker should discuss the original as well as revised goals and objectives, achievements during the helping period, factors helpful or obstructive in achieving the objectives, and the efforts needed to maintain the level of achievement and the feelings aroused by disengagement.

Follow-up is done to help the client maintain the improvement. During follow-up, the client is helped to discuss the problems he faces in maintaining the improvement. Work is done with the people significant for his improved social functioning. If required, he is referred to the proper source for needed services and help.

We have discussed various social casework approaches and it is up to the readers to choose their own model of practice. An eclectic approach or choosing the most suitable approach according to the nature of the problem is necessary to achieve the desired result. Though literature available on choice of approach in various types of problems is plenty, experience is the only key to choose the right approach in each case.

Crisis Intervention, Motivating and Skills

We have, so far, discussed the nature of casework and casework process. There are certain situations where knowledge of casework process and human behaviour do not suffice. Such situations in casework practice are crisis, and non-motivated clients who pose challenge to the practitioners. Dealing with such situations requires specialised knowledge and approach.

Crisis

From our experience of life, we all know that every person is subjected to various stresses, both internal or/and external at different stages of life beginning from childhood. One's ego develops only through learning to cope with such stresses and in this process one collects various coping devices and problem-solving techniques. These devices and techniques are usually sufficient to deal with the usual tasks of daily life. The problem arises only when internal and/or external pressures increase or the coping ability of the individual diminishes and in such situations one fails to maintain homeostasis, resulting in disequilibrium. According to Korner (1973), crisis may occur in two ways: *exhaustion crisis*, i.e., when the individual under prolonged stressful conditions suddenly reach a point where he fails to cope up any more with the stressful situation. Another is *shock crisis* which implies a sudden change in the environment resulting in excessive release of emotions that overwhelm his coping devices and render him incapable of perceiving, cognition and decision-making. Caplan (1951) sees a crisis occurring when an individual faces an obstacle to achieving his important life goals, which is for the time being, insurmountable by means of customary methods of problem-solving. He, like Korner, also sees various types of crisis situations precipitated by changes in the normal course of living such as leaving of home for boarding school by the child, birth of a baby, marrying daughter, unwanted pregnancy, retirement, ageing, rustication etc., and the situations, arising out of accidental and hazardous events like accidents, sudden serious illness, dismissal of the breadwinner of the family from job etc. Crises are seen usually as self-limiting and superimposed on normally functioning personalities. Intervention in these situations aims at "alleviation of the acute reactive condition without dealing with the underlying pathology".

Crisis situations requiring crisis intervention (1) in psychiatric settings are severe difficulties expressed by patients in their current living, social and emotional problems of alcoholics, suicide cases, families of alcoholics and psychotics etc.; (2) in medical settings, major surgery cases, acute and serious illnesses, families of such patients, etc.; (3) in family and child welfare settings, family feuds and violence, desertion by one spouse, sudden stoppage of income, immoral sex, pregnancy of an unmarried daughter, rape, running away of son/daughter, unexpected big expenditure etc., and (4) in community settings, disasters like flood, bombarding, storm, mass killings, mine blasts, dacoity, riots etc.

Crisis intervention has been the traditional concern of social caseworkers which is clear from the writings of Gordon Hamilton, Bertha C. Reynolds, Charlotte Towle, Helen Perlman, Max Siporin, etc. Traditional approach in casework and crisis intervention has something common as well as something different. Similarities are: (1) enhancing the ability of the person to cope up with the current problems in living, (2) intervention is for the specific problems of interpersonal conflict, role dysfunction and provisions for life, (3) it reaches only those conflicts which are either conscious or akin to conscious, (4) transference is recognised and handled, and (5) assessment of the client's position in family and community.

The differences are: (1) in crisis situations, unlike traditional casework approach, where social workers work very fast because of the urgency behind the problem, the client's willingness to take risk for regaining the sense of mastery and control over his life, and (2) quick decisions and actions in the role of advocate and activists are called for.

Crisis situations involve either threat to the instinctual needs, sense of well-being and autonomy or a challenge to mastery, existence and growth of individual or loss in terms of status, person, capacity, etc. It causes disequilibrium and disorganisation of self, followed by reorganisation and equilibrium. This period may last between a week to a month or so. During the reorganisation and reintegration period, ego picks up new adaptive styles and new techniques and becomes richer to tackle similar situations in future. This is usually possible with the help available from experts or experienced persons. Ego's self-confidence is fortified if it can tackle such situations effectively. The coping devices (the way people learn to adopt to and master internal and/or external pressure) learnt are new addition to its armamentarium.

It is recognised that, though anyone can come across with crisis situations, there is a population which is more vulnerable to such situations. Such a population is called "population at risk". With the "population at risk", public health approach, i.e., primary, secondary and tertiary intervention is advisable. While the *primary* intervention seeks to check "a potential situation from developing into a crisis", the *secondary* intervention aims at minimising the negative influence of the resultant equilibrium of the person experiencing crisis, and the *tertiary* intervention tries to check further deterioration and minimise the negative effects of the scars of the crisis.

Parad et al (1976) have suggested four basic steps in crisis intervention: (1) search for the precipitating event(s) and its meaning to the client, (2) search for coping means being utilised by the client, (3) search for alternate ways of coping that might better fit the current situation, and (4) review and support of client's efforts to cope in new ways and evaluation of results. Golan has suggested the following steps: formulation and assessment of the present situation, implementation and termination.

The caseworker, while assessing, should understand the hazardous event (a specific stress producing event), the subjective reaction (termed as vulnerable state also) of the individual or family to the event, nature of precipitating factors which heighten the tension or worsen the situation for the client, the state of active crisis (the subjective condition like psychological and physical turmoil and disturbance of intellectual functioning and of mood, etc., in the individual when his homeostatic mechanisms have become non-operative and disequilibrium, has occurred) and finally also how disequilibrium in earlier crisis situations subsided and with what advantage and disadvantage to the client in terms of learning new coping devices. Attempts should be made to understand the available supportive systems and the capacity of the client to deal with such situations.

After assessment, treatment goals are determined. These goals may be (1) relief from symptoms and checking the influence of precipitating factors, (2) restoration to the optimal pre-crisis stage of social function, and (3) locating remedial measures within the reach of the client and his family for tackling the situation. One may try to initiate new models of perceiving, thinking, feeling and adopting new responses. Though most of the techniques enlisted by Hollis (1972) and others are useful in helping the client, provision of protective (concrete) services and partialisation of the problem, involvement of the supportive social network and catharsis may prove more useful in crisis situations caused by sudden occurrence of hazardous events.

In the termination phase, one can review the tasks completed, new adaptive devices learnt, and the new mode of relating to persons and resources in the community. The caseworker in crisis situation has to be quite active, task-focused and committed to the client cause. He should remind the client about the time limit and the tasks completed after which the client has to move on the lead given by the worker.

Crisis situations in Indian settings are usually taken care of by the social network to which one belongs. People, as we know, are often recognised as groups based either on the lines of caste, religious sects or professions etc. The person in crisis is usually helped by the people of his own group. It has been observed that Indians by and large are more humane, probably because of their religion-dominated social life. Though it has been observed and reported that our social ties are weakening, recent increase in exploitation of masses for votes along the caste line seems to have checked this erosion to a considerable extent. Apart from this, communities in general, even in metropolitan towns, help their people in crisis situations. Such systems, if any existing in the community to handle crisis situations, need to be strengthened.

Reach Out and Motivation

One of the important problems not infrequently faced by social caseworkers in practice is to help a client lacking in motivation or exhibiting resistance to seek help. In such an instance of a *hard-to-reach client,* the caseworker in the interest of the client and society approaches (reaches out) the client with his help and services of the agency. This is seen more often in psychiatric set-up where they resent being hospitalised or examined by psychiatrists. Resistance of this nature is also common with the clients in correctional settings. These clients see their ego-dystonic (alien) behaviour as ego-syntonic (conducive) because of which they reject all help to get rid of their non-productive and non-congenial approach to life. In these cases of reaching out (*aggressive* casework) one uses advocating, persuasion, coercion and actual intervention or gifts (in terms of services offered by the agency) or social pressure to help the client to seek and use available services.

In many situations, some of these techniques may be considered either as unsuitable or undesirable. In such cases, motivating the client to utilise the services offered becomes very important.

Motivation or motive refers to the desire or emotion that moves one to act. Motives are the goals or objectives which we choose to pursue for our welfare and happiness. This impels us to act accordingly. These impelling forces may be either negative or positive. The positive ones are wants, needs, desires, etc., whereas the negative ones are fears, aversions, etc. These needs or wants develop, according to Maslow (1954) in a sequence, i.e., (1) physiological needs (hunger, thirst etc.), (2) safety needs, (3) belongingness and love, affection etc., (4) esteem needs, i.e., prestige, self-respect, and (5) needs for self-actualisation. Goals are different from wants. Goals are selected by individuals depending on their cultural norms and values, physical capacity, personal experience, availability of opportunities and resources. Wants and goals go on changing and developing which alongwith fears and aversion initiate and sustain behaviour of an individual. These wants and fears are subsumed under the term motive or need.

Swanson and Woolson (1973) tested their assumptions (selectively quoted below) about unmotivated clients. They say that to understand an individual's motivational pattern, one needs to know what rewards (or hope for rewards) have kept him behaving in the fashion he behaves. This can be discerned only when we note down his successes, satisfactions, failures, traumas, pains and the rewards he values more and his kinds of efforts to solve problems etc. They have, after their long experience of work and research, proposed that motivativation is likely to increase:

(1) if the patient can become actively engaged in setting his own goals for the outcome of therapy;
(2) if goals are definite, individualised and concrete rather than being vague, general and equally applicable to all humans. These goals should pertain to both the achievement of a new level of behaviour and of a new level of feeling by the patient;
(3) if we help the patient set priorities among his goals. This, of course, includes helping him set up a series of steps to be taken in a sequence. Also, it is often useful to help him distinguish between what he wants for his own comfort and survival as against what his family or intimate groups or community want from him;
(4) in proportion to the extent to which the patient believes he has a good chance of success (Maier, 1965). Review of his past satisfactions and successes helps caseworker formulate goals which have been within the reach of a person with his assets at one time, and presumably may be possible for him to achieve again.

There is evidence that psychiatric patients need more help than other people in setting for themselves goals that are neither too high nor too low (Heckhausen, 1967). There is also research evidence from several sources which indicates that being encouraged to set fairly high goals for oneself results in more achievement than does setting low goals (Rosen and D'Andrade, 1959; Coopersmith, 1967).

(5) if we help the patient become as aware of his habits of pursuing rewards as of his habits of avoiding traumas;

(6) if the patient is encouraged to indulge in fantasy about himself as he wants to be at the conclusion of the therapy and fantasy about both how he will be able to behave and feel after therapy. These need to be encouraged and rewarded;

(7) for psychiatric patients, as it does for students or workers, if regular feedback on result is provided (Maier, 1965); and

(8) if we help the patient restate his insights about his dysfunction into goal-oriented statements which are accurate for his individual situation.

Types of questions that might be used in attempting to help a patient understand his own unconscious goals and sources of motivation are being quoted below. These questions, according to Swanson and Woolson (1973), should not be used in direct, quick sequence but should be used gradually over a period of days after enough trust and rapport had been developed:

(1) What do you see as your main trouble now?

(2) Can you think for a few minutes about what have been the happiest times in your life? Will you describe these times to me and focus on your memories of some of them? What elements do you think have contributed to making these periods the most happy ones? How were these periods different from now?

(3) Of what are you most proud in your life, in yourself? List several. What is your job? How do you feel about it? What are the particular rewards and satisfactions of your kind of work? What are the particular disadvantages of this job? How do you feel about your employer, your immediate

supervisor, if any? How do you feel about the attitude of your company (or organisation) towards you? The union?

(4) How do you feel about the people who work with you?

(5) What changes would you like to make in your work situation? What obstacles have prevented these changes? Which of these could you change? How secure is your job? Are you carrying more than on job? Why?

(6) Have you children? What do you enjoy most about your children? What problems do you have with any of your children? What changes would you like to see in any of them? Do you want your children lives to be different than yours? In what ways? This is often the most productive question in uncovering repressed goals if patient is in a reflective mood and taking his time to answer.

(7) What do you like about your father and mother? What do you like least about your father and mother?

(8) How satisfactory is your marriage? What do you see as the main good points in the way your wife/husband treats you? Also, the main bad points? What are your own good points in relation to your marriage? Also, bad points? What changes would you like to see in your wife/husband? What improvements would you like to make in your treatment of your wife/husband?

(9) What sexual experiences have been most satisfactory for you? Why these particular ones?

(10) Can you describe your life the way you would like it to be? Let your imagination go freely. In such an imaginary picture, how would you feel most of the time? In what way is that different from the way you feel now? What work would you be doing? Where would you live? How would your living conditions be different than they are now? How would your marriage be different? Describe the kind of father/mother you would be? Describe exactly how you would make each of these choices? What changes would you like to see most in yourself? And also in your way of

living? In what ways would you like to change while you are in the hospital? Can you describe what kind of person you would like to be when you get out of the hospital (press for concrete details). If the answer is vague, i.e., I want to get well, one can point out that "getting well" means different things to different people. One may use examples from among patients on the ward, whom the client (patient) knows, in order to illustrate this, i.e. "for Mr. X getting well means being able to stop losing his temper and shouting at his children, for Mr. Y, it means feeling a lot more cheerful and active most of the time, and for Mr. Z it means being able to feel relaxed and happy without alcohol". Exactly what does "getting well" mean to you? One needs to encourage patient to describe with as much concrete details as possible.

We have talked your goals. What do you think now are the goals of some of the other people who are most affected by your behaviour, e.g., your wife, family, employer, people who work with you, etc. How do their goals fit in with yours? Are there some points at which their goals conflict with yours? Should we think about working out these conflicts between your goals and theirs?

Think quietly about yourself and your feelings over the past few years. At what times have your feelings been most pleasant, and satisfying? Can you describe what these feelings were like? What caused them?

Think quietly about your own feelings for the last few years. Try to describe very accurately the most unpleasant feelings you have had during that period. What caused these feelings? What feelings would you like most to replace them? What steps might be taken to make this replacement?

About what, have you felt most fear or anxiety during these periods? Specify it in the several years, and in the recent weeks. Have you outgrown the need for it? With what feelings would you like to replace it? What could be done towards making this replacement? What things have made you most angry during the last few years? Was this a pleasant or unpleasant feeling to you? To what degree?

Have you ever really solved the problem that made you so angry or does it continue to recur? What steps might be taken to solve it instead of enduring its recurrence? How did you behave when you were angry? Can you think of any other behaviour that might have been more effective or preferable?

Social caseworker then considers these points and use these questions to understand and enhance the client's motivation to utilise available services for his real help. Effectiveness of casework services rests on the individual's motivation, capacity and the opportunity he gets. To motivate him, his level of discomfort with the existing state of affairs will have to be increased by focusing on it, changing his values and definitions, creating fear of social criticism and loss, appealing to his family pride and assuring him of a better future alongwith extra doses of acceptance.

8

Models of Practice

The theoretical approaches discussed in Chapter 3 help us to explain motivating forces behind human behaviour and impact of social values, institutions and socio-cultural practices on it. Models of practice, on the other hand, discussed in this chapter tell us how to help the clients. While the former adds to our theoretical knowledge of human behaviour, the latter ones help us to learn and adopt the actual process to help clients in need of our expertise and help. The models usually delineate stages of the helping process alongwith objectives, activities and techniques to be followed. These models represent practice theories that deal with how to help and bring desired changes in the human behaviour.

One of the most commonly used practice theories is the one given by Family Service Association of America (1953), according to which casework treatment, based on goals, has been classified into two types: (a) to maintain adaptive patterns, and (b) to modify adaptive patterns.

Treatment Aimed at Maintaining Adaptive Patterns

This type of approach, ego supportive in nature, is indicated when the client needs help for restoration of or maintaining adequate functioning. The client is provided with realistic opportunities and experiences. This is aimed at supporting and strengthening various parts of ego functioning resulting in change of behaviour. Internal (personality) changes are not aimed at though it may occur as a by-product. Criteria for selection of clients for this category of treatment include (i) that the client has past record of appropriate adaptive capacity, has adequate motivation and average intelligence etc., and needs support for adequate functioning; and (ii) that the client is exhibiting unsuccessful adaption, severely impaired ego functioning and that he needs control of impulses. This implies that the functioning of the clients in the first category is temporarily impaired and that his adaption is unsuccessful in some major aspects of social functioning. Efforts are made to strengthen the existing defenses, to reduce/remove detrimental external factors to functioning and elaboration of new mechanism to maintain control. Work is carried at conscious level and with the present situation. Techniques recommended in this group are reassurance, informing, logical discussion, demonstrating, behaviour, advice and guidance, setting limits, ventilation, direct intervention and manipulation of environment.

Treatment Aimed at Modification of Adaptive Patterns

This approach, namely, insight-oriented casework, is used when the problem interferes severely with social functioning. As compared to socio-psychological problems, it is psycho-social in its nature. It seeks modification of selected ego-defense mechanisms in use. This approach is chased when the client (i) exhibits stereotyped (hackneyed) responses, i.e., his responses are not appropriate to the situation, and one type of response is repeated in most of the situations, and thus his responses are not individualised according to situation; and (ii) defense mechanisms are pathologically used. The ego must possess integrative ability---an ability to integrate various experiences and functions. Techniques used to achieve modification of adaptive patterns are confrontation, clarification and interpretation. These techniques help in developing insight to effect changes in the behaviour pattern of the client.

Perlman (1957) does not believe in any precise classification. However, she has presented her own scheme of solving the problems of the client. She sees problems in three ways as under:

Social Psychological

These problems are tackled by reassurance, support and environmental manipulation (tangible help and work with significant others on behalf of the client). These problems show in temporary impairment of functioning, weak ego, physical incapacity and lacking in external resources. The techniques are used to restore, maintain and improve functioning of the client.

Psychological Modification of Adaptive Patterns

Herein the goals are mobilisation, redirection and strengthening of ego's problem-solving functions which include perceptive, defensive, adaptive, integrative and executive functions. This is used with clients who show emotional capacity, normal intelligence, physical capacity and motivation (which is dependent upon the expression of discomfort and hope for its solution by the client). Techniques used in this group are relationship, identification, ventilation, support, advice, explanation and clarification.

Psychological Change of Personality

No attempt is made by the caseworker to change the personality pattern as he is not trained for it. Perlman's practice theory is known as problem-solving model. She pleads for maintaining relationship with the client on the basis of reality. Transference is received, identified and dealt with as it occurs. Problem-solving means "conscious, focused goal directed activity between the worker and client". Hallowitz (1967) adds "assertive counselling components" to make this approach more useful. These are: (a) *Crisis intervention*: Intervention in chaotic and critical situation to halt or reduce the unlimited destructiveness and to create a congenial atmosphere. (b) *Correction of disparities* between perception and reality. (c) *Dealing with discrepancies* between behaviour and goals. This is possible through clarification of the fact that the client's behaviour is self-defeating in the sense that it is blocking the attainment of the desired goal. (d) *Taking a position*: Wherever needed, the worker takes a stand on important issues and expresses his views honestly and politely. His (client's) requests for advice and guidance in such situations are entertained. (e) *Active direction-finding*: The caseworker discusses with the client to find, recommend or suggest the directions or objectives to be pursued by him though the decision always lies with the client. (f) *Direction-implementation*: Suggestions are given to implement the decisions and act on them in the decided direction. His motivation to act is fortified by substantial support, encouragement and recognition.

Hallowitz (1967), who has worked extensively on the problem-solving model of Perlman, cautions that the above six components are not a separate treatment modality but part of the problem-solving modality described above.

Task-Centred Approach

Developed by William Reid in 1970s, this model of casework, as discussed earlier, is a short-term and time-limited in its approach. The particular problem to be dealt with is decided mutually by the worker and client with an explicit agreement to a time limit (8 to 12 sessions within 2 to 3 months). Tasks or problem-solving actions are worked out collaboratively by the caseworker and client. The task may be to improve work performance or to undertake change in a certain behaviour. The caseworker helps him to carry out these tasks. Interventive procedures in this model may include anything between insight development and provision of social services. The problem is focused upon, and the specific tasks designed to solve the problem are accomplished. After exploration and assessment, the problem to be solved is formulated in terms of concrete actions (tasks) and they are executed within the stipulated period. The approach is used to deal with all psycho-social problems. All the techniques of casework are used in the same way as it is used in other approaches. The steps (activities) are as follows:

Problem-Specification

Problems are explored, and what the client really wants is deliberated. Clarification may be given about certain difficulties or consequences of the problem not in the immediate attention of the client. Problems are defined in concrete terms and usually in a single sentence. The problem of immediate importance is taken on priority. Causative, precipitating and reinforcing factors in biological, psychological and social fields are analysed.

Contracting

Verbal or written agreement is reached between the helper (caseworker) and helpee (client) on the specific problems to be solved, the kind of solution he wants, how frequently and how long they will meet, etc. This helps the client to think about the problem and its solution more clearly.

Task Planning

At this stage tasks are formulated and selected in collaboration with the helpee. Task means what the client is to do to mitigate his problem, e.g., to develop a plan to handle a truant or mentally sub-normal child, to develop a firmer and consistent approach to handle child's behaviour, or Mr. X is to apply for a job in a particular factory, etc. These tasks are nothing but a course of action. Alternative tasks (courses of actions) are also formulated. Tasks may be sub-divided, and priorities may be fixed in collaboration with the client. These sub-tasks are spelt out in terms of concrete actions that they will execute. It may be, for example, looking for advertisements, registration in Employment Exchange, etc., which all lead to solution of the problem. These are sub-tasks of the task to secure a job.

Incentives and Rationale

The purpose behind the task should be clear. Why this action, and what purpose it will serve are to be spelt out to the client. Consequences of actions should be realistically perceived by the client. Discussion of likely positive gains may work as incentives to work on the task.

Analysing and Resolving Obstacles

The problems likely to be encountered in carrying out the tasks are clarified and brought to the notice of the client. Obstacles when faced are critically examined. Obstacles may be either psychological or environmental or combination of these. Clarification of how these are thwarting the actions may help in removing the obstacles or revising the task.

Simulation and Guided Practice

The caseworker may demonstrate (or model) the possible task behaviour or ask the client to rehearse what he is going to say or do in certain situations. Modelling and rehearsal may be carried out to learn appropriate behaviour or actions wherein he is deficient. Guided practice is enacting the actual (as opposed to simulated) task behaviour by the client during the interview.

Task Review

What the client has and has not accomplished and what he has tried to do, are reviewed. This helps in devising way to handle obstacles, accelerate process of action, and revise the task or sub-tasks.

Terminating

Since time limit is set in the initial interview itself, the last interview is used to review the progress. The client is helped to think if he needs to work further on his problem, and if so, how will he plan to develop new tasks to be pursued by him independently. His achievements are underlined. Extension of services is usually not encouraged.

This model, though limited in scope, is useful for those clients who have fairly intact ego strength.

Austin (1950) has classified social casework treatment basically into two types: social therapy and psychotherapy.

Social Therapy

Goals in this therapy are to use social services and opportunities for better contacts with reality, and change the factors effecting the client adversely. This also seeks to preserve self-confidence and prevent the negative effects of accumulated strains caused by various stressful situations. Techniques are bringing change in the environmental factors (environmental manipulation) and use of resources (social and material).

Psychotherapy

Psychotherapy seeks to modify behaviour and attitudes within the existing personality structure. This has been further divided into three types: supportive, insight and experiential.

Supportive

It aims at prevention of further breakdown in clients whose ego is weak and who are vulnerable to further breakdown under stressful situations. Techniques included in this type of psychotherapy are reassurance, permissive attitude, protective relationship, use of social services and work with environment, clarification of reality issues, etc.

Insight

This therapy aims to achieve a change in the ego by developing patient's insight into his difficulties. Selected interpretations, reality clarifications, use of transference to understand the nature of impulses, and its sources, and how present differs from the past, and recall of relevant memories, etc., are undertaken to achieve insight into the nature and extent of feelings and the unconscious motivations behind them. Interpretations can be done in terms of how and why to bring the desired change. Interpretation helps the client to realise the undue influences of his parental ties and his childhood feelings on his current functioning.

Intermediate (Experiential)

It is blending of supportive and insight therapies with the central focus on the development and use of relationship as a corrective emotional experience. It means that the caseworker-client relationship experiences are directed in an orderly and conscious manner to neutralise the ill-effects of his experiences with the significant others in his earlier part of life. The caseworker's current relationship with the client helps him to review his earlier experiences and perceive them in the correct perspective. It loosens restructive ties to figures in the past by redirecting emotional energies, and also promotes growth through increased satisfaction in living. Change is sought in his adaptions within the current personality structure. In the case of a marital conflict, caseworker may use transference to trace his/her difficulties to his/her experiences with the parents in childhood and present himself as responsible parents (authority) to give the client a correct experience of authority figure and thus offset the negative effects of his/her earlier experiences with parents.

Austin is very near to the usual psychotherapist's approach with a lot of influence of psycho-analysis. This naturally requires, as she also suggests, special training and at least 3-5 years of experience in casework practice.

Psycho-social, a term in social casework, though originally a generic term, is now a very precise term and refers to a particular type of approach in casework practice. Precursors of this approach are Mary Richmond, Gordon Hamilton, Annette Garrett, Lucille Austin, etc. This term is said to have been used by Frank Hankins of Smith College in 1930. However, *psycho-social approach* (a practice theory) developed by Florence Hollis (1972) is now more accepted as a comprehensive approach in social casework practice. According to Hollis, social casework practice can be divided broadly into two types: (i) direct, and (ii) indirect. These are further sub-categorised into six and five types of interactions (i.e., range of procedures and techniques) respectively. However, the first four sub-categories are common to both the categories of direct and indirect. The common ones are: sustaining processes, procedure of direct influence, procedure of ventilation, reflective consideration of the current person-situation configuration. In the direct, two additional sub-categories are added, while only one is added to the indirect one. The two additional sub-categories in the direct casework are reflective consideration of patterns of personality and behaviour and their dynamics, and reflective consideration of the past and its effect on current functioning. The one sub-category added to the indirect casework is use of social service as discussed in Chapter 7.

Social Psychological Approach

Glynis M. Breakwell and Colin Rowett (1982) have presented the Social Psychological Approach (SPA). Opposed to individualist approach of psycho-analysis and behaviourism, this emphasises perceiving and understanding the individual in his social context. It neither ignores nor minimises the importance of the social processes which would give meaning to thought, feeling and action. It uses data and theories of social psychology. The approach observes the following model in helping the individuals in his environment:

Stage I: Analysis or Description

Herein the definition (or description) of the problem facing the client at each of the following four *levels* is examined:

(i) the intrapsychic---the thoughts, feelings and actions of each individual involved in the problem;

(ii) the interpersonal---the relationships between individuals involved;

(iii) the intragroup—the structure and processes of any groups involved; and

(iv) the intergroup—the relationships between any groups involved.

There are specific targets for description at each of these levels: (a) identity, (b) relationships, (c) groups, and (d) environment. These are the identifiable elements in the problems.

All these *targets* should be individually analysed at each of the four levels. For instance, an individual's identity process can be described in terms of intrapsychic dynamics, relationships, group membership, and relationships between groups that are important to the individual. In fact, this can be done for each target zone which means that the pattern of description can be very complex.

Level of Analysis or Description		*Target of Analysis*
Intrapsychic		Identity
Interpersonal	Each level can be used with each target	Relationship
Intragroup		Groups
Intergroup		Environments

This may involve the use of following information-gathering techniques widely used in social psychology:

(i) the interview;
(ii) observation, both participant and non-participant;
(iii) questionnaire and survey techniques; and
(iv) archival data, e.g., case histories, police records, community newspapers, etc.

Stage II: Explanation

Explanation involves understanding the processes which are involved in its genesis and its maintenance. We know that processes which cause the problem are not synonymous with those which maintain it. The social worker, in order to eradicate the problem, should be primarily concerned with the processes which maintain it since these are the processes which must be annulled or diverted if change is to be brought about.

The SPA finds the following four processes as central to all social behaviour and thus central to the social work problem as well: (i) construal, (ii) consistency, (iii) comparison, and (iv) conformity. These processes are used by many as the core of their explanations. One must choose from the different theories in order to explain the dynamics of the problem.

Stage III: Change

Various theories of human behaviour will indicate the features of the situation which need to be changed if the problem is to be ameliorated. The social worker may set up goals for change autonomously or in collaboration with the clients or other professionals. Once the goals are established, this approach would indicate that in order to achieve them the social worker must direct intervention at certain target zones (equivalent to the targets of description)----identity, relationships, groups and the environment. Altering the process of these target zones is the object of intervention.

The form of intervention will be shaped by knowledge of the way in which processes of construal, consistency, comparison and conformity control social behaviour. The social worker, informed by the theory chosen to explicate this particular problem, seeks to employ these processes to bring about change. Specific theories about the induction of personal and social change can be employed to direct intervention strategies.

Reflexivity

This is an orientation which should be adopted throughout the other three stages described above. Reflexivity is demanded of the social worker in the SPA. The social worker must be self-consciously aware of his or her own role in the problem and in the process of change. This awareness has two aspects:

(i) understanding the impact of the social worker on the clients and the problem dynamics; and

(ii) understanding the impact of the problem upon the social worker.

These two impacts are analysable in exactly the same way the problem itself is analysable through the use of levels of analysis and of explanatory processes. Since the social worker is often the very channel through which persuasion and coercion work to bring about the desired change in the situation, it is vital to understand how this channel works. It should be emphasised here that reflexivity does not refer simply to the social worker's understanding of himself or herself. It refers to an understanding of the "self in interaction with others while in the occupational role of social worker. This is very different sort of understanding from awareness of the 'self' in a vacuum".

Before understanding the process, meaning of various terms used in it need to be explained. *Identity* is identical with self-concept. It is continually changing rather than static entity. It entails awareness of our separation from others and the uniqueness of our consciousness. It is a social product and is located in a social context. It carries our expectations about ourselves. It is only through social interaction that we develop our identity—personal as well as social. *Relationship* includes (i) how people form their impression of others when they first meet, (2) what leads people to like or dislike others, and (3) how long-term relationships develop. Under the target, *group*, SPA understands (i) nature of groups, (ii) intragroup dynamics, i.e., the nature of group membership, the importance of norms and conformity process, group decision-making, and leadership, and (iii) intergroup dynamics, i.e., explanation of conflict and cooperation between groups and reducing intergroup conflict. *Environment*, i.e., physical environment can (a) be a determiner, a problem or it can mediate the determination of a problem, (b) be manipulated for amelioration or solution of the problem, (c) act as a context to the analysis of the problem and thereby influence the conclusion drawn, and (d) influence the way in which the client perceives the social worker and his/her actions. SPA model seeks change in attitude and behaviour to help the client through the process of attitudinal change, persuasion and coercion. The key processes that need to be considered in explanation of an event/problem are:

(a) *Construal process* is the way in which people make sense of the happenings and people around them. It includes assimilation of information, categorising these as per one's experience, and giving it meaning. It tells how we see, what we see, and how we think about responding to the world around us.

(b) *Consistency* implies maintaining one's thoughts, feelings and actions in a state of equilibrium. Inconsistencies between any of these result in problem for self and weakens one's ability to predict experience and its understanding. It harmonises the present thinking with the previous experiences.

(c) *Comparison* is used by us to validate our understanding of the world. Value, a social construct of any person, depends upon how he/she fares in comparison to other persons. Comparison is a continuous process. We assess our position relative to others. Comparison leads to differentiation (efforts to make oneself distinct in valued ways). Differentiation brings in personal and social change because when old differences diminish, new differences emerge.

(d) *Conformity* means that (i) we need social approval necessary to maintain self-esteem, and (ii) we enforce conformity upon others.

(e) *Explanation* of the problem in terms of construal, consistency, comparison and conformity.

(f) *Intervention* in order to generate change, techniques based on the motive power of construal, consistency, comparison and conformity.

The SPA approach will be explained from a case-record given by Breakwell and Rowett (1982).

Vedantic Approach

Upadhyay (1993) has propounded the Vedantic approach to solve individual problems. Its main components are described below:

1. *Listening*: This is the first step in solving problem of anyone including self. The worker should listen to client and client should listen to worker. Listening (*shravan*) involves a rapt attention on part of the both as we find in the *Gita*. This includes verbal as well as non-verbal communication without which understanding of the event and person remains incomplete, and therefore, faulty. The content of listening can be all that the client or worker wants to talk about the person, problem, situation and its causes as perceived by them.
2. *Self-study*: Wherever needed, the worker and client both should study about the problem and its solution. (We do have reading for fieldwork as part of our practical training). If both of them study relevant literature, it sharpens their

thinking and equips them with pertinent knowledge to solve the problem and help the client. *Swadhyaya* helps in acquiring right knowledge of the subject (problem-situation) as advocated by Jains. These two steps can be treated as part of study.

3. *Intellectual reflection (Manan)* : Perlman (1957) says that problem-solving starts in the mind of worker. Vedantis treat this step as a separate and meaningful stage in finding answer to the problem and related questions. This step involves introspection to locate possible reasons within self (personality) and its contribution to the problem and reasoning over various causative factors (external and internal) to weigh their relative strength, and to find out alternative solutions. This may involve clarification of doubts through mutual consultation and discussion between worker and client. (These steps, in terms of social work language, mean working with the client). *Manan* involves reasoning over the relevant and the irrelevant, relationship between various factors, meaning behind these factors and their role in causation of the problem, the appropriate solutions methods to be used and beliefs (faith) to be substituted. It is through reasoning that one gets the right views of the problem-situation as outlined by Buddhists. This helps in perceiving various aspects (angles) of the person-problem situation as contained in the principle of 'Anekantvad' (of Jains) which means that every situation is multidimensional, and that to arrive at correct decisions, one should discern all the dimensions of the situation and object.

   Though it is mentioned as a separate step here, it does occur in every problem-solving effort as opined by Perlman (1957). How much time (sessions) is to be spent on these activities will depend upon the gravity of the problem.

4. *Detection of causes*: Once the worker and client have gone through these processes, they can reach and locate the real

causes for the problem. These causes can be either spiritual, bodily or physical. Spiritual includes supernatural forces beyond our control, causing flood, fire, drought, death, etc. Bodily includes physical and mental faculties and physical (*bhautik*) includes problems and sufferings caused by non-living beings including animals etc. Detection involves the question of perception of the world and its events and their effect on the client (*Gita* 38, *Yogvashisth* 3/40/13). *Yogavashisth* also mentions that all the problems are caused by our ideas and faulty style of life. The modern literature also mentions these psychological truths.

Since *manan* and *kārak* are very close to each other, one may like to put them together as *karak-manan*, the assessment phase of social casework.

Negation: Swami Chinmayanand, in his commentary on *Gita* (1980), mentions this step which involves contesting and resisting the ideas and desires which are unrealistic and which create, activate and reinforce the problem-situation. Lord says: "Empty thyself, I shall fill thee." This calls for discarding the problematic desires/ideas (*Gita* 6/12). RET also advocates disputing the beliefs. This will be feasible only when we have gone through the first three stages and have realised the abominable nature of the beliefs (faith) behind our desires and actions.

Freud talks of resistance to the uncovering of unconscious. According to psycho-analysts, resistance is linked to underlying defense mechanisms against impulses from the id that are threatening ego. In negating the abominable beliefs also, one experiences resistance from within as it involves discomfort. Dr. Radhakrishanan (1948), while commenting on *Gita* (2:7), also says similar things: "It is general experience of seekers that they are assailed by doubts and difficulties even when they are on threshold of light." The light as it begins to shine on any soul provokes the darkness to resist it. The struggle with darkness will continue until the light fills one's whole being.

6. *Substitution*: The process of educating Arjun in *Gita* is to help him to discard his unrealistic ideas (beliefs) and substitute them with more realistic ones to enable him to perform his role. Adler (1963) also says that psychotherapy is an educational process which involves changing values.
7. *Repeating*: Lord Krishna tells Arjun that one can achieve if someone really wants to achieve something only by repeating the efforts (*Gita* 6/35-36). Substitution of any idea (or action) is hardly possible unless the effort is continued till the new ideas (values) replace the old (unrealistic) ones. It is only through repeated efforts that one can achieve what one wants to achieve. There is no other way out (*Yogvashisth* 3/6/14). Company of good people helps in accelerating our efforts (*Yogvashisth* 2/16/11) to modify our lifestyle in accordance with the realities. Wherever the problems are due to lack of material resources, concept of charity is helpful. However, charity (*dānam*) should be given to only those who deserve it as judged from their social situation, personal conditions, the period and place of the events (*Gita* 17/20: *desh*, *kal*, *patra*). This is in conformity with the view of social work profession. The social worker is not only enabler, but a catalyst, and a resource person also.

So far as the techniques are concerned, the caseworker can use the techniques of various schools of social work and psychotherapies in addition to the ones used in our scriptures, as described in the earlier pages (Chapter 1).

Integrated Model of Practice

In the recent years, thinking in social work profession has shifted from the traditional approach of casework, group work and community organisation to an integrated approach or an *unitary* model of practice. This change has found wide acceptance in USA, and a large number of schools of social work there have changed their curriculum accordingly.

However, in India, this model is yet to make a dent into social work practice. Goldstein (1973) finds traces of unitary model of practice in the paper, "A Working Definition of Social Work Practice" prepared by NASW in 1958, and social work curriculum study by Boehm in 1959. Compton and Galaway (1975) quote Schwartz (1961 and 1970) and Bisno (1969) who question the validity of social work practice in the traditional model. Pincus and Minahan (1970) wrote that some schools were introducing unitary concept of practice in their curriculum. The reasons, put forward by Compton and Galaway (1975) against the use of traditional model of casework, groupwork and community organisation, are: (1) it is based primarily on the size of the client system (in which the social worker intervenes), rather on activities utilised by the worker; (2) it encourages the dichotomous approach of changing the individual or the situation rather than focusing on the person-situation interaction; and (3) it has also resulted in a tendency to see problems in terms of the methodological skills of workers rather than in terms of complete assessment of the client-situation interaction. Others plead for integrated model because they find a common core of knowledge, skills and techniques behind these three methods of casework, group work and community organisation and regard these as unnecessary segmentation.

The integrated approach (or unitary model) takes care of these points as it focuses on "the transactions of individuals and their environment with both individuals and environment in a constant state of reciprocity with each shaping the other". This model is more consistent with ecological approach. This integrated approach in social work, in lieu of casework, groupwork and community organisation methods, uses knowledge of general systems theory, communication, role, ego psychology and psycho-analytic constructs.

Goldstein (1973) has presented his unitary model consisting of the following phases:

1. *Role induction phase*, when the focus is directed towards the clarification, development and assumption of the client role concurrent with the identification and evaluation of the problem or task.
2. *Core phase* is that juncture when the change system is stabilised, emphasis is placed on problem-solving capabilities, and efforts are directed towards resolution and change.
3. *Ending phase* is the terminal phase of service wherein resolution of the problem or task is achieved and evaluated. Consideration is given to subsequent planning.

Like this, various authors have proposed their own set of phases in the unitary model of practice presented by them. For example, Compton and Galaway (1975) have suggested a model of practice based on the assumptions that (i) people want to control their own lives and to feel competent to master the tasks they see as important, (ii) motivation for change rests on some integration between a system's (individual or group) goal and its hope-discomfort balance, (iii) the social worker is always engaged in attempting to change some interactions or transactions within or among systems, (iv) systems are open and the input across their boundaries is critical for their growth and change, (v) while a system must have a steady state for its functioning, it is constantly in flux, and (vi) all human systems are purposive and goal seeking.

The outlines, after assumptions of the model, given by Compton and Galaway (1975) is quoted here to apprise the readers with the model as such. The author expects the practitioners to use these outlines selectively, as certain outlines may not be useful in some cases. Thus, one may not need all the informations suggested in these outlines in detail. These outlines have been selectively presented herewith with the belief that the readers, after having read and understood casework process, will be able to follow these outlines and try it in their practice if they so desire. If more details of the model is required, they can refer to Goldstein (1973) and Compton and Galaway (1975).

Outlines of Problem-Solving Model (Compton and Galaway, 1975)

Contact Phase

I. *Problem Identification and Definition*
   A. Problem as the client system sees it:
      1. Significance and meaning assigned by the client system to need, lack or difficulty.
      2. Nature and location of need, lack or difficulty.
      3. Length of existence, previous occurrences, precipitating factors identified.
      4. Conditions that bring client system and worker into interaction at this time.
      5. Significance and meaning assigned by the client system to this interaction.
   B. Problem as defined by significant systems with which the client system is in interaction (family, school, community, others):
      1. Nature and location of need, lack or difficulty as seen by these systems.
      2. Significance and meaning assigned by these systems to this need, lack or difficulty.
      3. Significance and meaning assigned by these systems to client's interaction with interventive agent.
   C. Problem as the worker sees it:
      1. Nature and location of need, lack or difficulty.
      2. Precipitating factors that the client system knows about and believes to be related and that the worker knows about and believes to be related.
      3. Significance of conditions that bring client system and worker into interaction.
      4. Nature and degree of effort that client system has put into coping with problem and client system's feeling about such efforts.

D. Problem-for-work (place of beginning together):
   1. Problem or part of problem that the client system feels most important or a good beginning place.
   2. Problem or part of problem that in the worker's judgement is most critical.
   3. Problem or part of problem that falls within the action parameters of the helping system.

II. *Goal Identification*

A. How does the client system see (or want) the problem to be worked out?
   1. Short-term goals
   2. Long-term goals.

B. What does the client system think is needed for a solution of the problem?
   1. Concrete resources.
   2. Specific assistance.
   3. Advice, guidance or counselling.

C. What does the client system see and/or expect from the agency as a means to a solution?
   1. Specific assistance (concrete service to enable the client system to do something).
   2. Specific resources (concrete things).
   3. Change in the environment or other social systems.
   4. Change in specific individuals.
   5. Advice or instruction.
   6. Support or reassurance.
   7. Change in self.
   8. Change in interaction between client system and others.

D. What are the worker's goals as to problem outcome?
   1. Long-term goals are different from client system's goal?

2. Short-term goals are different from client system's goals?
3. Does worker believe client system's goals to be realistic and acceptable?
4. What facilitating and intermediate goals can be identified?
5. Level of agreement between worker and client system on goals.

E. What does the worker believe the service system can or should offer the client to reach these goals?

1. Specific assistance.
2. Specific resources.
3. Change in the environment or other social systems.
4. Advice or instruction.
5. Support or reassurance.
6. Change in self.
7. Change in interaction between client system and others.

III. *Preliminary Contracts*

A. Clarification of the realities and boundaries of service.

B. Disclosure of the nature of further work.

C. Emergence of commitment or contract to proceed further in exploration and assessment in a manner that confirms the rights, expectations and autonomy of the client system and grants the practitioner the right to intervene.

IV. *Exploration and Investigation*

A. Motivation

1. Discomfort.
   - (a) Quantity and quality of discomfort.
   - (b) Is discomfort generalised to total life situation?
   - (c) Is it attached to present situation?

(d) Is it focused on presenting problem?
(e) How much discomfort is attached to help-seeking or help-taking role?

2. Hope
(a) Quality and quantity of hope.
(b) Is there a generalised quality of optimism based on evaluation of past successes in coping?
(c) Are past experiences separated from present situation with realistic perception of the difference involved?
(d) Does client system perceive means of dealing with problems that are acceptable and does client system perceive ways of access to such means?
(e) Gratifications from efforts towards solution including relationship to worker, other critical systems and resources.

B. Opportunity

1. What opportunities have there been for client system to experience success in coping?
2. What feedback has been available to client system as to value of these successes?
3. What opportunities have there been for client system to acquire knowledge and skills needed for coping with present problem?
4. What part of present problem is a result of departure from average level of opportunity made available to individuals, families and groups in present society?
5. What opportunities for solution of problem does the worker see in the present situation?
(a) Socio-economic.
(b) Within individual, family or group as primary system.

   (c) Within family, group, or community as secondary sources.
   (d) In worker's skill, service system and community or outside resources.
   (e) Others.

C1. Capacity of the Client System

1. Factors in the study and evaluation of the individual in any system: dyad, family, small group, organisation or community.
   (a) Physical and intellectual
      (1) Presence of physical illness and/or disability.
      (2) Appearance and energy level.
      (3) Current and potential levels of intellectual functioning.
      (4) How one sees one's world, translates surrounding events---perceptual abilities.
      (5) Cause and effect reasoning and ability to focus.
   (b) Socio-economic factors
      (1) Economic factors: income level, adequacy of subsistence, and way it effects lifestyle, sense of adequacy and self-worth.
      (2) Employment and attitudes about it.
      (3) Racial, cultural, and ethnic identification: sense of identity and belonging.
      (4) Religious identification and linkages to significant value systems, norms and practices.
   (c) Personal values and goals
      (1) Presence or absence of congruence between values and their express in action; meaning to individual.

  (2) Congruence between individual's values and goals and the immediate systems with which the individual interacts.
  (3) Congruence between individual's values and those of practitioners (meaning of this for interventive process).

(d) Adaptive functioning and the response to present involvement
  (1) Manner in which individual presents self to others (grooming, appearance and posture).
  (2) Emotional tone and changing levels.
  (3) Communication style (verbal and non-verbal, level of ability to express appropriate emotion, to follow train of thought and factors of dissonance, confusion, and uncertainty).
  (4) Symptoms or symptomatic behaviour.
  (5) Quality of relationship individual seeks to establish: direction purposes and uses of such relationships for individuals.
  (6) Perception of self.
  (7) Social roles that are assumed or ascribed, i.e., competence with which these roles are fulfilled.
  (8) Relational behaviour
    (a) Capacity for intimacy
    (b) Dependency-independency balance
    (c) Power and control conflicts
    (d) Exploitative
    (e) Openness

(e) Development factors
  (1) Role performance equated with life stage.
  (2) How developmental experiences have been interpreted and used?

(3) How individual had dealt with past conflicts, tasks and problems?

(4) Uniqueness of present problem in life experience.

C2. **Factors in the Study and Evaluation of the Family**

(a) Family as a social system

(1) Family as a responsive and contributing unit within the social network.

(i) Family boundaries: permeability or rigidity.

(ii) Nature of input from other social units.

(iii) Extent to which family fits into cultural mould and expectations of larger system.

(iv) Degree to which family is considered deviant.

(2) Roles of family members

(i) Formal roles and role performance (father, child, and so on).

(ii) Informal roles and role performance (scapegoat, controller, follower, decision-maker).

(iii) Degree of family agreement on assignment of roles and their performance.

(iv) Interrelationship of various roles, i.e., degree of 'fit' within total family.

(3) Family rules

(i) Family rules that foster stability and maintenance.

(ii) Family rules that foster maladaptation.

(iii) Conformation of rules to family's lifestyle.

(iv) How rules are modified and respect for difference?

   (4) Communication network
      (i) Way family communicates and provide information to members.
      (ii) Channels of communication, i.e., who speaks to whom.
      (iii) Quality of messages, i.e., clarity or ambiguity.

(b) Development stages of the family
   (1) Chronological stage of family.
   (2) Problems of and adaptations to transition.
   (3) Shifts in role responsibility over the time.
   (4) Ways and means of problem-solving at earlier stages.

(c) Sub-systems operating within the family
   (1) Function of family alliances in family stability.
   (2) Conflict or support of other family sub-systems and family as a whole.

(d) Physical and emotional needs
   (1) At what level does family meet essential physical needs?
   (2) At what level does family meet social and emotional need?
   (3) Resources within family to meet physical and emotional needs?
   (4) Disparities between individual needs and family's willingness or ability to meet them.

(e) Goals, values and aspirations
   (1) Extent to which family values are articulated and understood by all members.
   (2) Do family values reflect resignation or compromise.
   (3) Extent to which family will permit pursuit of individual goals and values.

(f) Socio-economic factors as outlined in earlier paragraphs.

C3. Factors in the Study and Evaluation of Small Groups

(a) Functional characteristics

(1) How group came to be (a) natural group, (b) group formed by outside intervention.

(2) Group's objectives

(a) Affliative, friendship and social groups: mutuality and satisfaction derived from positive social interaction; tendency to avoid conflict and to stress indentification.

(b) Task-oriented groups created to achieve specific ends or resolve specific problems, i.e., emphasis on substantive rather than affective content.

(c) Personal change groups---emphasis on psychological and social content-dynamics of interpersonal behaviour.

(d) Role enhancement and developmental groups: recreational, educational and interest clusters and emphasis on rewards and on gratifications of participation, observation, learning and improved performance.

(3) How group relates to contiguous groups, how it perceives itself, and is perceived as conforming to or departing from outside values.

(b) Structural factors

(1) How the members were selected and how new members gain entry?

(2) Personality of individual members

(a) Needs, motivations, personality patterns.

(b) Homogeneity-heterogeneity.

- (c) Age of members.
- (d) Factors of sex, social status and culture that relate to functions and purposes.
- (e) Sub-groups, their reasons for being, and the purposes they serve.
- (f) Nature and locus of authority and control
  - (1) How leadership roles develop?
  - (2) How decisions are made?

(c) Interactional factors
- (1) Norms, values, beliefs, etc.
- (2) Quality, depth and nature of relationships
  - (a) Formal or informal.
  - (b) Cooperative or competitive.
  - (c) Freedom or constraint.
- (3) Degree to which members experience a sense of interdependence as expressed in individual commitments to the group's purposes, norms, and goals.

C4. Factors in the Study and Evaluation of Organisations

(a) Organisation as a system with mandate:
- (1) Organisation's task: its mission within the social structure
  - (a) Clarity with which task is stated.
  - (b) How task is perceived by organisation's members?
- (2) Individual and group roles relevant to the task
  - (a) Which persons have the responsibility for carrying out the mandate of the organisation?
  - (b) Elements and parameters of their roles.
  - (c) Congruence between expected role behaviour and how these roles are seen by role bearers and others.

- (d) Are roles assumed, delegated, earned or appointed?
- (3) Location of organisation within system of organisations
  - (a) Population group, organisation is designed to serve.
  - (b) Kind of problem for which it is accountable.
  - (c) Organisation's isolation from or cohesion with other organisations.
  - (d) Quality of inter-organisational communication.
  - (e) Way organisation manages input from other systems.

(b) Culture of the Organisation

- (1) Style with which organisation operates
  - (a) Governing beliefs of members.
  - (b) Expectations and attitudes of members.
  - (c) Theories that govern and guide organisational activities.
- (2) Mode of interaction with external groups or within organisation itself
  - (a) Formal or informal.
  - (b) Deference to authority—hierarchical.
  - (c) Ritual.
  - (d) Channels of communication.
- (3) Organisation's technologies: resources, methods, and procedures in implementation of organisation's task
  - (a) Jargon.
  - (b) Routine and protocol.
  - (c) Accepted and approved modes of communication.

(c) Competence of the organisation
  (1) Availability and adequacy of funds, physical plant, equipment.
  (2) Scope of authority vis-à-vis the community.
  (3) Special status, force, and control in relation to larger community.
  (3) Merit of guiding policies, flexibility and responsiveness.
  (4) Efficiency of internal decision-making process.
  (5) Level of morale, spirit of commitment of members.
  (6) Degree to which above factors combine to make the organisation more than the sum of its parts.

C5. Factors in the Study and Evaluation of a Community
(a) Community as a social system
  (1) Organisations, institutions, and groups of the community which affect existing condition and how they are linked with the another.
  (2) Location of the problem and community units related to it.
  (3) Units that can be engaged to deal with the problem: their stake in change and their accessibility.
  (4) How will change in any one unit affect other units?
(b) Community as an organic entity
  (1) Attitudes towards social control and conformity.
  (2) Opportunities for social mobility.
  (3) How the community defines success or failure?

(4) Beginning appraisal of the community power structure and how it exercises controls.
(5) How power is achieved in the community?
(6) How prevailing problems are identified and by whom?
(7) Beliefs held about causes of social problems.
(8) How the community labels the victims of social problem?
(9) Problem-solving capacity and resources.

(c) Inter-community structures and processes---relationships and regulations within governmental and non-governmental sectors.

Contract Phase

V. *Assessment and Evaluation*

A. If and how identified problems are related to needs of the client system?
B. Analysis of the situation to identify the major factors operating in it.
C. Consideration of significant factors that contribute to the continuity of the need, lack or difficulty.
D. Identification of the factors that appear most critical, definition of their interrelationships and selection of that can be worked with.
E. Identification of available resources, strengths and motivations.
F. Selection and use of appropriate generalisations, principles and concepts from the social work profession's body of knowledge.
G. Facts organised by ideas---ideas springing from knowledge and experience and subject to the governing aim of resolving the problem and professional judgement.

VI. *Formulation of a Plan of Action: A Mutual Guide to Intervention*

A. Consideration and setting of a feasible goal

1. Goal is set, as the direct results of, and during the process of, problem definition and analysis.
2. Goal should be mutually agreed upon and within a set time limit.
3. Goal should be within the capacity of the community, client system and worker to achieve, given the opportunities the environment can offer, the worker's resources and skills and what the client system can bring to bear.

B. Determination of appropriate modality of service.

C. Focus of change efforts

1. Client system (what particular aspect of functioning?).
2. Family system (what aspect?).
3. Significant others in the client system network.
4. Agencies and other institutions in the community.
5. Worker's own service system.

D. Role of the worker

1. *Advocate*: when legitimate resources are resistive or resources must be created.
2. *Broker or mediator*: locates resources for client system, interprets client system's needs to others, attempts to modify others' behaviour towards client system, and mediates between client system and others.
3. *Teacher*: provides information, explanations and expressions of opinion and attitudes, models effective behaviour.
4. *Enabler*: attempts to help the client system to find within the system itself and the system's situation the necessary answers and resources by communication

of interest, sympathy, understanding, and the desire to help; encourages explorations or ventilation of content concerning the nature and interactions of the client system and the client system's situation; encourages the reflective consideration, awareness and understanding of the present person-situation-problem gestalt; plans with the client system; and encourages the client system to act independently.

5. *Therapist*: makes communications that contribute to or encourage reflective consideration, awareness, and understanding of the psychological patterns and dynamics of the client system's behaviour; or aspects of the client system's earlier experiences that are thought to be relevant to such present behaviour; or aspects of the person-situation gestalt that lie in the past.

E. Consideration of forces in or outside of the client system that may impede the plan.

F. Consideration of the worker's knowledge and skills and of the time needed to implement the plan.

VII. *Prognosis:* What confidence does the worker have in the success of the plan.

Action Phase

VIII. Carrying out of the plan—specific as to point of intervention and assignment of tasks, resources and services to be utilised, methods by which they are to be used; who is to do what and when.

IX. *Termination*

A. Evaluation with client system of task accomplishment and meaning of process.

B. Coping with ending and disengagement.

C. Maintenance of gains.

X. *Evaluation*

A. Continuous process.

B. Was purpose accomplished?

C. Were methods used appropriately?

In the end, another model of social work practice, i.e., generalist approach, similar to unitary model, developed by Louise C. Johnson (1983), also deserves a brief description to acquaint the readers with this important development in the field.

In social work, though services like assistance in problem solving, therapeutic services, developmental services (group work in community centres), crisis intervention and concrete services like income maintenance (old age pension etc.) are provided, social work does not consist in the services but in *how* the services are rendered (i.e., the approach) and what is the focus of the services. Social work's focus is on social functioning, an interaction "between the coping activity of people and the demand from the environment".

Johnson identifies two different aspects of the social workers approach: (i) worker's interaction with individuals and social systems while focusing on social functioning and also while providing services, and (ii) the process of serving. Components of the interactional process are the worker and client interacting in an environment. This interactional process is understood differently from the process of serving or work ("for purpose of study" only). Interaction and serving (work) are considered as ways of looking at the "professional response to need" of the client.

In the *interaction* process, Johnson discusses (1) worker's self-knowledge, responsibility and authority, helping skills and the worker as a helping person; (2) becoming a client, understanding the individual client and family as a multi-person client; (3) formation of a one-to-one action system, relationship, communication and interviewing, (4) small group as a social system and social worker as a member of group; and (5) environment which includes the community as a social system, agency as provider of service and worker as an employee of the agency.

In the work process or *service* process, Johnson includes and discusses only four processes, viz., assessment, planning, action and termination. He includes study or exploration in the assessment phase which comprises (1) investigation, collection and exploration of information, (2) identification of the needed information, and (3) decision-making about the information needed. Decision-making involves interpreting meanings, ordering informations and discovering relationships among different parts of the situation. The planning phase embodies formulation of goals and objectives, deciding unit of attention, strategy, roles, tasks and techniques. Action contains use of resources, crisis intervention, mediating, use of activity and work with 'chaotic family'. It also includes action with others on behalf of the client which involves use of 'influential' to bring change, mobilisation and development of resources, environmental manipulation, organisational change and advocacy of the client's cause. Termination discusses disengagement process, accountability and its relationship to evaluation as an ongoing activity to review the plans and action concurrently.

Two new approaches are emerging on the international social work scene. One is *evidence based practice* and another is *capacity building*. Capacity building combines the empowerment and development models of social work. It enables people and communities to solve their own problems and thus effect significant and lasting change.

In spite of these innovative changes in social work approach, writings on casework continue to increase in USA and UK. To me, unitary model makes little difference because one, while using this model with an individual becomes more of a caseworker and similarly a group worker when working with a group. Integrated method, of course helps in one way, i.e., the worker does not get weaned away from the other methods of social work and he can use his knowledge of other methods in helping his clients. Need for frequent referral may get reduced. He becomes more of a generalist than that of a specialist. I am still in favour of specialising in a specific method. In an era of specialisation, being generalist is somewhat out of tune. And I think that perhaps this is the reason that questioning of effectiveness of casework by Joel Fischer has hardly any effect on its use by "tens of thousands of social workers in a wide variety of social service and other institutions. Whatever its limitations, work with individuals...is widely used... In a sense, it is the mother of methods" (Skidmore and Thachery, 1982). Timms (1964) is also critical of generic approach when he says: "It is fashionable in social work at the present time to decry specialisation...". However, what approach a social worker should adopt to serve his clients ought to be guided by the question: how far the objectives can be served by a particular approach. One has to be flexible and eclectic and not adherent to one school or approach and modify his tools to suit the purpose and the objectives to be achieved.

9

Social Casework and Other Helping Professions

Social workers employed in medical and psychiatric settings face a lot of difficulties because of role ambiguity and role confusion. The employers and members of medical/psychiatric team are not fully clear of the capacities and skills of social worker. Not infrequently social workers are put to executive, non-professional jobs. Apart from other factors, our training system and government policy on delivery of medical/psychiatric services play major part in compounding this confusion. During the training period, social workers should be made fully aware of their skills, *vis-à-vis* those of medical and psychiatric personnel. The knowledge, approaches, skills and techniques, which are common and shared by other professions, should be clearly spelt out. Against this backdrop, the present chapter delineates the nature of differences between social casework, psychotherapy, counselling and family therapy.

Psychotherapy, in the words of Wolberg (1954), is a form of treatment for problems of an emotional nature in which a trained person deliberately establishes a professional relationship with a patient with the object of removing, modifying or retarding existing symptoms, of mediating disturbed patterns of behaviour, and of promoting positive personality growth and development. It is to alter the behaviour and change the attitudes of maladjusted persons towards a more constructive outcome. It may be said to be a planned programme for modifying the emotional life and adjustment of the patient through new life experiences resulting from the encounter between the therapist and patient. Since emotions and behaviours are dependent upon, and generated by thinking, a successful therapy seeks a cognitive reorganisation resulting in change in the behaviour of the patient.

Psychotherapy has been further classified by Wolberg into three types: (a) supportive, (b) re-educative, and (c) insight therapy. *Supportive psychotherapy* is applied to strengthen existing defenses, to reduce or remove detrimental external factors that act as or produce stress, to elaborate new and better mechanisms to maintain control, and to restore emotional equilibrium. Techniques used in this type of psychotherapy are guidance, environmental manipulation, externalisation of interests, reassurance, pressure, coercion, persuasion, emotional catharsis, desensitisation, prestige suggestion, etc. *Re-educative psychotherapy* helps in developing insight into more conscious conflicts, in readjusting, and in living up to the existing creative potentialities. Relationship therapy, attitude therapy, psychobiology therapy, counselling, casework and reconditioning are included in this type of psychotherapy. *Insight psychotherapy* seeks development of insight into unconscious conflicts with efforts to achieve extensive alteration of character structure. New adaptive potentialities are developed and help is rendered in expansion of personality. It seeks restructuring of personality. The techniques used in this therapy are those of psycho-analysis, like free association, hypnoanalysis, narcotherapy, clarification and interpretation, etc.

As discussed earlier, casework was, first of all, given a systematic treatment in Mary Richmond's work, *Social Diagnosis*, in 1917. Her work set forth the principles of social investigation and gather all significant facts to know the client's personality and his situation. Before her, the caseworkers dealt with the problems and not the individuals. Problems like desertion, alcoholism, poverty or illegitimacy were treated. 'Indeed there was a well-known worker who approached all unmarried mothers with a pocket full of wedding rings.'

In this era of moral conformity, when the history-taking aspect of social casework treatment was dominant, Freud's theory of personality 'burst like atom' and the case history which was largely sociological became 'psychosocial'. Knowledge and understanding of the child's bio-psycho-social growth process revolutionised ideas of family relationship and of interaction.

The id, ego and superego became not only usable in understanding behaviour, but essential in focusing treatment. Caseworkers now began the slow uphill climb to practise clinically with therapeutic aims and tools that were 'to change the profile of social work'. Social work heavily drew upon psycho-analysis which is still very much influencing the social casework practice. The emphasis on manipulation of the parents for the child's good (in child guidance clinics) shifted towards psychosocial treatment of the parents as clients. The work of the neo-Freudians, such as Sullivan, Horney, Fromm, etc., supplied an important cultural orientation.

In addition to these, there was enormous effect of Otto Rank's thoughts on social casework which resulted in a school called 'functional' as against diagnostic school based on Freudian thoughts mainly. Social casework, as we have discussed earlier, "intervenes in the psychosocial aspects of a person's life to improve, restore, maintain, or enhance his social functioning by improving his role performance. Intervention occurs when the persons or members of his group, community, realise that his role performance is hampered or threatened. The intervention takes place through a professional relationship between the worker and other individuals whose interaction with the person affects his role performance. Since social functioning is the product of interaction among intrapsychic, somatic and social forces, social casework involves assessing the internal and social factors which impair or threaten the person's role performance and helping him to find and use the somatic, psychic and social resources at his disposal, to eliminate or reduce malfunction and to enhance functioning in social roles" (Boehm, 1959).

The GAP Report No. 2 (1948) defines psychiatric casework very much as psychotherapy except for a heavier emphasis on external reality and social conduct. Grinker and others (1961) have outlined the following functions of psychiatric social workers in a psychiatric clinic: (i) exploration, (ii) information, (iii) recommendation, (iv) experiencing complementary relationship (supportive psychotherapy), (v) modifying complementary relationship (insight psychotherapy).

Various typologies of social casework treatment were given by Bibring, Austin, Mass, Perlman, Hamilton, etc. However, we will briefly mention the two typologies of casework treatment (discussed in chapter 8) given by Family Service Association of America (1953) and Hollis (1972) which are currently followed by the majority of professional social workers. According to Family Service Association of America, work/treatment is of two types. One is supportive which aims at maintaining adaptive patterns, and techniques included in this group are manipulation of environment, reassurance, persuasion, direct advice, guidance, suggestion, logical discussion, use of authority and immediate influence. The other type of casework aims at modification of the adaptive patterns through the techniques of clarification and interpretation.

Hollis, in her book, *Case Work: A Psychosocial Therapy* (1972), classifies casework treatment in two types. One is direct, and another is indirect. Processes and techniques used in the direct type of casework treatment are: (a) sustaining procedures which are dependent upon demonstration of interest, desire to help, goodwill, understanding and reassurance; (b) direct influence which includes suggestion, advice, advocating and intervention; (c) catharasis; (d) reflective consideration of the current person-situation configuration focused on (1) the situation which includes people, conditions, events, (2) decision and consequences, (3) inner awareness, responses, distortions, and (4) reactions to the worker and to treatment; (e) reflective discussion of the dynamics of the response patterns or tendencies; and (f) reflective discussions of the genetic development of behaviour patterns or tendencies.

All the first four groups of techniques mentioned in the direct treatment are common to the indirect type also and the fifth group of techniques in the indirect casework treatment is provision of protective services such as financial assistance, placement, employment etc. (see chapter 7).

The casework deals with conscious and pre-conscious material and not with the unconscious part of the system. The caseworkers who deal with unconscious part are having training and supervision by psychoanalysts. Casework process is more rational and less directive and it works *with* the patient and not for the patient. Casework has its objective to steer "change to occur in the individual(s) or in the situation or in both". And, the delivery of service—the meeting of a concrete need is used as a "tool in treatment".

Grinker and others (1961) commented on the relationship between casework and psychotherapy that "a definite and irreversible trend has slowly emerged, placing the psychiatric social workers among the professional psychotherapists. Our position has been that the social worker should perform all psychiatric social work functions including psychotherapy".

Parad (1958) mentions that the dichotomy of the individual versus environment is a deceptive one and social work adopts "person-in-situation" approach.

A leading authority in casework practice, Hamilton (1951) mentions: "The characteristic casework method is interpersonal and combines both psychological and social therapies. For more than twenty-five years, casework has practised its distinctive form of psychotherapy, and, at its best, continues to make use of all the familiar social services as social therapies."

Rapoport (1969) has written that it is a "blending of psychological understanding and management with social provision, thus giving us a wide and rich range of choice in the instrumentation of the change process".

Casework can be differentiated from psychotherapy at the following points (when the author talks of psychotherapy, he invariably refers to Wolberg, 1954).

Level of Consciousness

As stated above casework techniques always address to the conscious and pre-conscious material and never attempt to explore the unconscious part of the personality. However, if any such material is brought out to the surface by the client on his own, caseworker may utilise it in helping the patient. Many times, dreams may be used beneficially, though casework does not extend itself to understand the unconscious significance of dreams and symbols. He may interpret it as it relates to conscious and pre-conscious materials.

In psychoanalytically-oriented therapy and psychoanalysis, the emphasis is on, as Wolberg (1954) describes, bringing out unconscious conflicts to awareness. In re-educative psychotherapy, the emphasis is on pre-conscious materials. And, because of this *similarity* between casework and re-educative therapy, Wolberg (1954) has categorised casework in *re-educative* group of psychotherapies.

Nature of Techniques

Some of the techniques considered to be specific to casework are:

1. Reaching out the persons in need of help who do not seek help on their own, or who resist help.

2. Home visiting.
3. Rendering concrete services. Caseworkers have responsibility to locate community resources, both financial or institutional, and help the patients to use them to their benefit.
4. Interpretation is common to both casework and to psychotherapy in nature and process. In casework, it is the pre-conscious materials and not the unconscious material which is interpreted.

Social casework uses all the techniques of supportive and re-educative psychotherapy.

Types of Problems

Caseworkers may not always work with psychosocial problems, but simply help their clients to tide over their present critical periods, thus restore their social functioning. Psychotherapists focus on the problems of emotional nature, usually on the symptoms of the emotional problems.

Objectives

Unlike psychotherapy, caseworker's objective is to enable "change to occur in the individual, or in the situation or in both". Sometimes, the change in situation is specifically directed to bring change in the individual. In casework, unlike in psychotherapy, transference is never encouraged, though positive transference is utilised for promoting growth and negative transference is controlled and if necessary it is analysed in the context of corrective relationship (in terms of reality).

In psychotherapy, the objectives are either bringing change in the individual behaviour and attitude, or restructuring personality (altering character structure) of the patient (client). It can now be summarised that social casework, in terms of psychotherapy (as enumerated by Wolberg, 1954) can be said to be consisting of supportive and re-educative psychotherapy plus social services in terms of concrete assistance (provision of services).

Counselling

Counselling is a process to assist the individuals in understanding himself *vis-à-vis* his situation and problems, in exploring alternate solutions, in taking most appropriate decisions in the situation, and in enhancing his capacity to solve problems independently. Counselling is not possible without rapport and effective communication. No attempt is made in counselling to go deeper into the personality pattern of the counselee. The system of study, assessment, goal formation, treatment planning, treatment and termination of social casework is not followed in counselling. Interviewing techniques of counselling are the same as are used in casework. Unlike the caseworker, the counsellor never tries to understand genetic and dynamic factors; his main focus is on "the current person-situation configuration" only. Counselling also enables the counselee to solve his future problems on his own, i.e., it leads to self-counselling. The counsellor like the caseworker works with the counselee to adjust to the situation though he never tries to change the situation of the counselee. The counsellor neither undertakes home visits nor renders concrete services. In recent years, many changes have occurred in counselling and many use it as a synonym of psychotherapy while others consider it as a process to help the counselee "to understand all the accumulated data about himself in the context of his world and to develop the ability to take wise, discreet, independent and responsible decisions" (Dave, 1983).

After discussing the differences between social casework and psychotherapy, and counselling, an attempt will be now made to understand family therapy and its relation with social casework.

Family Therapy

It is treatment of a family in conflict. The whole family is helped to see and appraise their relationship with each other and the unhealthy current reactions to one another are resolved. The individual is seen in the context of the family and is helped to perform his roles and bring changes in his relationship with others in the family. Re-ordering of relationship or restructuring the interaction pattern of family members is aimed at in family therapy. Modification of family interaction to restore and strengthen the adaptive and equilibrating forces resulting in reorganisation of family (its members) roles is undertaken and focused in family therapy. It is only a clinical orientation, a modality and not a treatment method, which uses different therapeutic concepts. It seeks to restore and improve social functioning, restore equilibrium, strengthen adaptation, meet emotional needs and maximise development of the individuals in the family. The goal in family therapy may be an alteration in the family interactive pattern, promote changes in the system (family), a shift in the interaction of intimates, or a re-equilibration in the family functioning to enable it to promote its members' development and meet their needs appropriately and adequately.

In family therapy, the therapist may start either with individual members or the whole family or the dyad (couple). It is up to the therapist to choose his way of intervention. Some may see individual members followed by whole family, while others may start with the whole family or dyad followed by individual sessions with family members. The individual who seeks help for his problems is usually seen individually in the first instance followed by family sessions. Family therapy is neither casework nor group work. It has elements of both the methods.

The *case* of an adolescent was referred to the author for stealing household things from his own house and indulging in black-marketing of cinema tickets. While talking with the client, I (author) found that the family itself was functioning pathologically. Parents of the client had hardly any relationship except that they lived under the same roof and the mother cooked the food. The physically handicapped sister extended help to everyone. The youngest child, an agent (ally) of the father, tried to dominate the domestic scenes. The client was troublesome to both the parents. The problem of the client was seen as manifestation of the family interaction. After initial interviews with the client, the whole family was seen in three sessions while the client was seen by psychiatrist. The sessions were devoted to observe and appraise the family interaction pattern and necessary shifts in the interaction style was introduced through advice and discussion. After a week of this intervention, the father reported a 'wonderful change' in the family function.

In family therapy the therapist sees individuals not only as individuals but also as members (parts) of a larger whole (family) interdependent of each other and together forming a bigger system, i.e., family. Individual problems are seen as expressions of malfunctioning of the family, therefore, intervention is planned at the family level. Rebellious behaviour, poor school performance, running away from home, etc., are not only problems of the individuals but these reflect something wrong in the family. In this therapy we find a clear linkage between social therapy and psychotherapy. Many a time two therapists join and conduct the family sessions together or one may see the individual member concurrently with the family session. To practise family therapy one needs a better understanding of system approach, role theory, communication theory and small group behaviour, along with developmental aspects of family. This will help in integrating the modalities (family sessions and/or individual sessions) and knowledge for family therapy. Such an integrated approach focuses on the family system and process, sees family as a whole (its values, aspiration, behaviour and defenses) and at the same time, tries to grasp the meaning of individual experiences. Thus techniques of both casework and group work are used depending upon the unit of interaction.

The approaches, modalities (seeing individuals or dyads or whole family) and techniques used in family therapy are varied though the goal is the same. Theoretically, two models viz., *systems* and *structural*, are prominent in practice but it is difficult to discern them in real practice. As mentioned earlier, an eclectic or integrational model has found acceptance with the practitioners. This model looks at the homeostatic behaviour of intimates, the nature of hierarchical structure, and developmental changes in the lifecycle of natural groups like family, etc. In recent years, *two* major approaches have assumed importance in family therapy. In one approach, a small change in the system is introduced and amplified to restructure the family interaction. In another approach, a crisis is introduced and the family is helped to reorganise itself. One of the important precaution is not to side with any member or section of the family.

In casework, when two or more members of a family need help, each person is helped on individual basis. Casework with family (or family casework) has in the last two decades gained importance in social work practice. It is synonymous with family therapy. Like family therapy, in social casework with family, (1) the whole family is seen as a social unit, (2) the focus is on what and how the family members communicate (verbally or non-verbally) with each other, (3) the relationship patterns between various sub-units (i.e., between spouses, spouses and children, and among the siblings) are observed and guided in the real sessions, (4) assessment is done to see who is the scapegoat, provocateur, healer, spokesman etc. in the family, (5) various family conflicts, destructive relating patterns, communication failures and formation of sub-groups (or pairings) in the family are identified, (6) members are made aware of inadequacies in the communication pattern, and the areas of failures in family functioning like caring of the child, old parents etc., and (7) needs of various units and individuals are discussed along with ways to reduce tensions and non-productive behaviour patterns, and thus the social caseworker works, as a change agent to repair, improve or change the family functioning (the family structure). Two caseworkers may join to work as co-therapist, and more than one family (conjoint) may be involved simultaneously in the treatment process.

Now, it should be clear that in the social casework process individuals are the focus of attention, and, others if involved, are to help in the restoration/improvement of the client's social functioning. In family therapy or social casework with family change is sought in the whole family as well as in the client.

10

Case Records: Discussion of Casework Process

In this chapter, case records have been reproduced. The first case is that of a probationer. This explains the process of social casework usually practised in correctional and other settings. Comments have been given in the parentheses ( ) wherever required. The second record requires knowledge of a new approach, viz., social psychological process (explained in Chapter 8). The whole SPA process has been explained with the example of a case. This model also proceeds through the same basic stages of helping though it uses different concepts to analyse the situation and a mixture of techniques from casework as well as from different psychological therapeutic schools.

Social Casework Record from Correction*

Name of the client: Ratan (name changed)

Age: 14 years

Sex: Male

Religion: Hindu

---

* The author is grateful to Prof. C.P. Goel, Dean, Faculty of Social Work, Kashi Vidyapith, Varanasi for this record. This is a process record of work (edited) of a 4th semester student of M.A. (Social Work).

Referral: The case was assigned by the lady probation officer for treatment of the problem of delinquency, truancy and disobedience.

Agency Background

The probation officer provides supervisory and correctional services to juvenile and youthful offenders released under the State First Offenders & Probation Act (repealed now) after having been found guilty of an offence by a court of law. Only such offenders who have been convicted for the first time of an offence, and are below the age of 24 years at the time of commission and are not charged for an offence punishable with life imprisonment or death, are eligible to be released under the Act, if the sentencing authority, not below the rank of First Class Magistrate, is satisfied that such release is desirable in view of the circumstances, age, etc., of the accused. The release is on probation, on condition of good conduct with or without supervision. The cases in the agency are referred when the release under the Act is with supervision. The period of probation is determined by the court and is to be between one and three years. Only in some cases a pre-sentence inquiry is conducted, otherwise in most cases courts on their own initiative release offenders on probation and are placed under the supervision of the probation officer. Social history, in many cases, is not available.

In this case, the client was on probation for one year under the supervision of a lady probation officer. The case had been in contact with the probation officer for some time when this case was assigned to the worker.

Background of the Case

The client was an adolescent boy, charged for theft/pickpocketing and was brought before the court. The client being first offender and of tender age, was released on probation of good conduct for one year. His father stood surety for the case and was responsible to the court and to the probation officer for custody, upbringing and education of his son and was subject to general supervision, guidance and control of the probation officer, who in this case was an elderly, but a professional probation worker with orientation in social work.

The client was studying in class VI, and was not regular in attending school. The parents felt that he was a shame to the family and were growing sick of him. The father went to his shop in the morning and returned late at night and so was true of the elder brother. The family was joint, medium-sized, consisting of father, mother, elder brother, sister-in-law (wife of the elder brother), client, a younger brother and a younger sister. The family lives in a part of a rented house situated in a congested locality. The locality was composed of heterogeneous elements, people of different economic classes and backgrounds.

The parents had cordial relations amongst themselves. The mother had a dominant role in family affairs and the elder brother was indifferent to the case. The sister-in-law was reported to be hostile to the client. The father was erratic in his discipline of the client whereas the mother was lax. The client has started feeling that his father was not interested in him as he used to scold him for his misbehaviour and truancy from school.

Worker's Impression

The family was conscious and well aware of the status of their son being a probationer. They were very eager for the treatment of his misbehaviours. They harbour a fear that the client could be sent to prison if they did not abide by the suggestions of the probation officer (including the worker), as failure to come to his expectations might result in conviction of the client. This resulted in submissive behaviour of both the client and his parents to the suggestions of the worker.

Record of Interviews of the Worker

January 4

The worker went to the probation officer and reported to her that he was back from his vacations and requested her to assign him a case. She discussed a few cases and referred the case of Ratan. She told that Ratan was an adolescent boy coming from a middle class family and was a problem both at home and school. He was charged for pickpocketing and indulging in acts of delinquency, e.g., stealing, disobedience and truancy from school and home. She explained that the family of the case was interested in seeing the child reformed and was cooperative. She gave the worker the home address of the client and advised to see him early next morning.

January 5 (Home Visit)

The worker called at the residence of the client. An elderly lady came out and asked the worker his identity. The worker introduced himself as a student of social worker in probation office and that the lady probation officer had asked him to help Ratan in solving his problems. He added, "I am interested in Ratan and will be ready to help him and his family in solving Ratan's problems" (identity and purpose explained in brief). She took the worker inside her house and offered him a seat. Showing her concern for the visit of the worker, she commented, "I am completely sick of Ratan and his behaviour. I am unable to decide what to do with him. Ratan refuses to listen to them, sells away household articles, runs away from classes, wanders in the company of vagrants and stays outside home for most of the day".

The worker was listening quietly and assured her that he would try his best to help him (no false hope) and explained how with his contacts with Ratan and with their cooperation he could be helpful. She felt somewhat assured and willingly requested him to do something for them. The worker said,

"Please do not worry much about this ('worry' is not the appropriate word) as such problems among children are not uncommon (knowledge given). Children do change and improve by careful and intelligent handling. Your cooperation in this is much needed". She at once replied, "I have done every thing for him and I am willing to do for him whatever is suggested. You will never find me failing in this. Ratan is, after all, my child and I want to make him a good boy". The worker said that she was quite right and enquired what plans she had for him (exploration). She replied that she wanted good education for him and was also ready to spend necessary money for this. The worker supported her saying that she was kind to Ratan and her concern for his welfare was praiseworthy (recognition). The worker told her that he would see her next Wednesday if she liked and also asked her if he could see Ratan. At this she pointed out to a boy (Ratan) standing near her and said that she would welcome the worker whenever he cared to come. She went upstairs leaving the client to the worker. Ratan had remained silent during the conversation with his mother, was rubbing his face with hands and was uneasy which was, but natural, due to her criticism of him (observation).

Interview with Ratan

The worker asked Ratan how he was but without any response. He further said to him, "I will be glad to help you if you have any problem". He kept silent for a while and hesitatingly remarked, "I have no problems" (denial by client, direct reference to problems creates resistance). The worker asked him if he could say why he had been convicted (too early to ask it). He narrated his conviction story saying, "One day I had gone to see a friend at his residence. His parents had gone to picture leaving him alone at the house. My friend asked me to stay for sometime to give him company and I agreed. After two hours I returned home. On this day my friend's father has left Rs. 70 in his coat pocket in the room where we had been sitting. When his father returned, he found the money missing and asked his son about it. His son showed his ignorance. His father asked him if any outsider had come to the room during the day. He told his father about my (clients) visit that day and emphasised that I was a good boy and he could not expect me to be a thief. I was called by my friend's father and to his inquiry I expressed my ignorance of the money. He reported the theft to police who charged me for theft. The court released me on probation."

After this the client became quiet. The worker showing his concern remarked, "This must have been a painful situation for you" (empathising). The client felt supported, emphatically said, "Of course, and the same thing is pinching me till today". "We don't like people who mistrust others," the worker further added. He replied in affirmative and felt a sense of relief. He added, "I have now stopped going to my friend's house". The worker accepting it said that every friend could not be like that. He said it was true that in order to avoid danger of further trouble he had decided not to go to any friend's house, though he remained with them in school and market and talked to them. The worker supported him saying that he did well in exercising control over himself and he looked pleased and comfortable (underlining). The worker asked him if he should come next Wednesday and he agreed to it wilfully (no negative points discussed).

January 9

As the worker approached the house to meet the client, his mother came out and told that client was present upstairs. She told the worker that he had spent away his school dues and has been absenting from the school for the last three days. He also wandered in the company of vagrant boys of the locality. The worker told her that he would talk to Ratan and will work with him so that he goes to school (a realistic assurance).

The worker went upstairs and found the client sitting on floor in a sad mood. The worker asked him, "Ratan, why are you sad? Will you share your feelings with me?" "I have done a very wrong thing", said Ratan, "I spent away the school fee and did not attend classes. My parents are annoyed with me. It is all due to my friends who pressed me to spend money on them. The headmaster struck off my name." The worker told him if his name had been struck off, it was his responsibility. "I will never squander away the fee again. I am extremely sorry for that. I can assure you, if I am readmitted to school, I will study hard and will never give any one a chance to complain", told Ratan. "Please do request my parents to get me readmitted to school, I am really sorry for what I did" (the so-quick realisation of his mistakes by the client appears to be more because of spade work done by court, parents and the probation officer who had already initiated him to think of solving his problem which had not taken deep roots till then. The empathic understanding and concern shown by the worker quickened the process of realisation).

The worker, learning of his interest in study, assured him that he would give all help in this connection and asked if it would be convenient for him to accompany him to school just then to find out facts (to verify if he is really interested). Ratan readily agreed and accompanied the worker to school (confirms client's interest in readmission).

School Visit and Interview with the Teacher

On reaching school, both the worker and the client met the class teacher of the client. The worker introduced himself as a student social worker interested in the client. The worker requested the teacher to tell his opinion about Ratan's performance in school. The teacher told that Ratan was good at studies but was not paying attention to his studies and so his performance was growing poorer every day. The worker asked what possibilities the client had in class. The teacher said to the worker if Ratan was readmitted, he could get through the examination because he was of normal intelligence and could continue his studies. The worker requested the teacher for his help in the readmission of Ratan. The teacher assured to provide all necessary help in this connection. The worker thanked the teacher, told him that he would be visiting soon and left the school (this shows the interest of worker in the client). The worker asked the client to talk to his parents about his readmission in the light of the talk of this day. The client promised to do so.

January 16 (Interview with Client)

The worker called at Ratan's house and asked him if he was permitted to go to school. He told that his parents did not want to get him readmitted to school at that time as they had decided that he would join next July or new session. The worker asked him about his plans. The client expressed his desire to continue studies and was anxious to get readmitted immediately. The worker decided to discuss it with his parents and asked his consent. The client readily agreed to the proposal.

Interview with the Parents

The worker went to the client's parents and after formal talks he explained the object of his visit. He enquired of them what plans they had for the education of Ratan. The mother told that he had been absenting from school quite often, now that his name was struck off, and he was quite weak in studies, they felt that he should continue his studies privately at home and should join some good school next year. The worker told them the opinion of the class teacher (information giving) and also the wishes of the client. He added, "Ratan is perhaps not so weak in studies. Now he understands his situation. Once he has suffered due to his irresponsible behaviour, he is likely to learn from this. As the teacher has promised help and I am also here to guide and instruct him, so why not accept what he wants and get him readmitted to school. He has sufficient time left for the final examination and it is better not to waste one year" (explaining). The father replied after a pause that he had no objection to Ratan's readmission and was ready to provide facilities. The worker appreciated them for this decision and told them that he would be coming next week to accompany Ratan to school for readmission (a gift to the client).

January 23 (Interview with Ratan)

Ratan, after wishing the worker, told that he was waiting for him. The worker asked him if there was anything which he could also share. He replied in affirmative and told that the previous day he had a quarrel with his sister-in-law (elder brother's wife) because she usually abused him at the time of lunch and many a time refused to serve him lunch. The worker suggested that she might have been joking but he emphatically protested saying, "She is jealous of me and hates me". The worker told if it was so, he would also talk to his sister-in-law and he hoped that she will change her behaviour (working with significant others). The client felt assured. Then, the worker asked if he was ready to go to school that day.

He replied that on the last Friday, a day after his last visit, he had decided to go alone to his school for his admission and had asked his father for school fee. The father had scolded him and had refused to give him the money. They had told that he would go to school with the worker. He further added that probably they did not trust him and that is why they had refused to give him money. The worker said that in his opinion it was not so (the worker should use "might not be" as he is not sure) because they had full sympathy with him and always cared for him and if they had no feelings for him, they would have totally refused for his readmission (drawing his attention to the other side of the situation). The client accepted that the worker was right and he (client) had misunderstood his parents. The worker assured him that all was in his favour and there was nothing he should bother about and he would be admitted to school that day. He felt reassured and nodded in confirmation.

On worker's asking, he got ready, got fees and accompanied the worker to school.

Interview with School Principal

The worker introduced himself and wanted that Ratan be admitted to school. The principal complained about Ratan's misbehaviour in school, and expressed hesitation to admit him as he would spoil the whole class (the worker should have talked to the principal during his first visit to school). The worker explained Ratan's problems telling him that he was changing and he hoped that he would not commit in school any misconduct which would prove him to be a source of trouble for them. The principal with hesitation agreed to admit Ratan, and so Ratan was readmitted to school. The worker expressed his gratitude to the principal for this act of kindness and both client and the worker returned to Ratan's house. As the worker was getting late for his agency, he told Ratan that he would see him again next week, and he agreed to it. The client expressed his gratitude and greeted the worker.

January 30 (Interview with Mother)

After exchanging wishes, the worker asked her whether Ratan was going to school. She told that he was going to school regularly, and also that he was improving in his bahaviour, adding that he listened to her, behaved well and worked hard in study. She expressed her gratitude to the worker for his help. The worker said that she need not thank him because it was a part of his work. The worker was also informed by her that Ratan had left the company of his 'bad' friends and they too were not coming to him. Then, the worker asked her to tell him something about the client's past behaviour and since when they had found him misbehaving. She told that he was a good student upto the age of 11 years but after passing class V he was admitted in Bengali Tola Higher Secondary School for further study. His father had engaged a tutor to teach him at his own residence and Ratan used to go to his teacher for studies. One day Ratan stole the teacher's fountain pen and the teacher complained this to his father and the father enquired about it. At first Ratan plainly refused if he had taken the fountain pen but when his father punished him, beating cruelly, he admitted his fault and returned the fountain pen. After that he never went to his teacher. The worker suggested that it might be that it was the root of Ratan's misbehaviour and suggested her if his father, instead of beating, had enquired about the matter intelligently, this problem might not have arisen. He suggested her not to scold or punish him in future, but should make him realise the situation by reasoning and sympathetic attitude. She agreed to do so in future.

Then, the worker enquired whether Ratan had been studying at his own house after he had left going to tutor. She replied in negative explaining that from that day they had found a change in his behaviour. He had started beating his siblings without reason and had stopped going to school and never studied at home. The worker told her that she had narrated a very important incident of his life which would be very helpful in solving his problems. Then, the worker told her that he would talk more about this some other day as Ratan was seen coming (insecurity of worker). The mother left.

January 30 (Interview with Ratan)

Ratan greeted the worker and asked when the worker had come. The worker told that he had come about half an hour earlier and was talking to his mother (honesty). Then, the worker enquired from Ratan of his well-being asking him how he was. He informed that a piece of glass had pierced into his foot and he had been attended to in Marwari Hospital. The worker expressed sympathy and asked if he was absenting from school due to this. Ratan replied that he was regularly attending school and was also going to hospital for bandage. The worker praised him for his courage, devotion and supported him by saying that he did well and he must care for his health and education (encouragement). He seemed pleased and comfortable. The worker then asked about client's feelings towards his parents but surprisingly enough he told that his parents were kind to him and supported him to their level best and he was proud of them. The worker appreciated his ideas and said that his parents are really interested in him and always had best wishes for his welfare and progress, and the client endorsed it. The worker suggested to meet him next Wednesday and he agreed.

February 6 (Interview with Ratan)

Today, the worker saw him studying. The worker greeted him and enquired about his treatment. He told that he was completely cured. The worker enquired how his study was going on. He said that he was going to school regularly and was also working very hard at home, and he further added if the worker did not trust him, he could ask his school teacher or his parents. The worker hearing this at once said that he had full confidence in him and there was no need to ask the school teacher or parents. The client seemed pleased with this. The worker asked him if there was anything new. He said that all was going well. As the client was busy in his homework, the worker thought it better not to disturb him and told him that he would meet on Wednesday next (follow-up to 'reinforce' his gains).

February 13 (Interview with Mother)

The worker greeted her and asked about Ratan. She said that Ratan was not present as she had sent him to purchase tickets for cinema as they were going to see a picture that day. The worker enquired if Ratan's school was closed that day. She told that he had not gone as he was also eager to go to picture with her. She seemed somewhat apologetic and defensive. The worker asked if it was in Ratan's interest to be absent from school (making her aware). She expressed her regret and assured not to repeat it. The worker requested her politely not to do so in future explaining her that this practice could be harmful to him as he would be absent from school in order to see pictures. She accepted my suggestions.

February 13 (Interview with Ratan)

The worker met Ratan at cinema hall and after exchanging greetings, he enquired why he had not gone to school. He replied that that day his mother and he were in a mood to see 'Sampuran Ramayan' as it was its last day. The worker asked if it was wise to see pictures absenting oneself from school. He said he was sorry for it. Then, the worker asked if he knew how it could harm him (drawing his attention to the consequences). He replied that the teacher would again scold him as well as would complain against him, and finally the principal could strike off his name from school. The worker asked why should he do such mistakes which could prove to be a cause of trouble to him. He said that he was extremely sorry for it and he would not absent himself from school in future. The worker appreciated it. The worker fixed the next interview.

February 20 (Interview with Ratan)

The worker found Ratan studying in his room and appreciated him. He told that he had completed his home work and had shown to his class teacher and he had praised his work. The worker said that he was working very very hard and his success was sure, if he continued (reassurance). The client said that his class teacher was very nice to him and the worker accepted it saying that he too was influenced by him at the time of his conversation. In the meantime, his mother came and the worker greeted her cordially.

Interview with Mother

The worker asked her if Ratan had become a 'good boy'. She replied that the worker was right as Ratan was obedient, well-behaved towards them, and was also sincere and industrious about his study and did not go out in the company of 'bad' friends, and whenever he went outside the house he took permission from her. The worker said that it was only due to her attention and proper care (recognition). She seemed pleased. The worker further added that though she had tried to help him to be good, but had failed to take care of his needs. Now change in his behaviour has been facilitated by their care of his needs and love shown. She seemed pleased and we agreed to talk the next Wednesday.

February 27 (Interview with Ratan)

The worker greeted him and asked about his well-being. He said that he was alright and that he was feeling better in contrast to past days; further commenting, that he was not expecting this sort of change in his life. The worker told that everyone has a right to grow and change and there was nothing impossible if one tried. He agreed to this. Then, the worker asked him if there was any problem which still remained, he would be glad to help him. He said that he was alright and thanking the worker said that he had done a lot for him and he would be ever grateful to him for this act of kindness. The worker said that he need not thank him because it was a part of his duty which he did.

Interview with Mother

The worker greeted her and informed that as she knew, it was worker's last visit to them, and if she had to say anything about Ratan, she was welcome. She said that they were quite well and thanked for the help rendered by the worker. It was possible due to their valuable cooperation and enthusiasm and concern for the child, said the worker.

Interview with Father

The worker also greeted Ratan's father and informed that he was not coming any more because the problems of Ratan had been solved and now he was in a position that he could help himself. He said that the worker had done much for them, commenting that they could not forget him for his acts of kindness. The worker said that all this was possible due to their pain-taking and valuable cooperation. The father asked the worker to take a cup of tea as this was their last meeting. At first, the worker told that there was no necessity of formalities but on his insistence, he took tea and returned to his agency.

Case History of Herbert (quoted from Breakwell and Rowett, 1982)

Herbert had been seen wandering about the fields, sleeping rough in sheep huts or in cow barns. He seems to spend most of his time muttering to himself, is generally unkempt and is reported as having a wild look about him. He is currently sleeping in a pig shed, and the wife of the farmer who owns the pig shed has complained to the police that he takes no notice of her when she asks him to move away, merely continuing to mutter and staring in the opposite direction. The local police constable visited the scene, and considers that Herbert is "man as a hatter". He has managed to elicit the man's name from documents in his pockets, and has found that Herbert does not have a police record. The constable has contacted the local SSD (Social Service Department) with whom he has a good relationship, and asked that a social worker be sent to make an assessment. The duty social worker checked that the SSD had no records on Herbert, and subsequently visited the scene. For some reason, the social worker finds Herbert in a talkative mood, and Herbert explains that he is staying in the pig shed because the pig shed is his property. He is married to the farmer's wife, and he owns the land. The wife wants him off the land because she had developed a relationship with the man she currently calls her husband, but who in fact is not. They are conspiring to deprive him of his property. The lady in question denies Herbert's assertion resolutely. Herbert looks verbally aggressive but there seems no reason to believe that he might be physically violent to anyone. After an amount of discussion, Herbert agrees to spend the next few days in a hostel run by the SSD. During this time, he behaves in a manner acceptable to the hostel warden, and takes the opportunity to clean himself up. He still mutters to himself and is resolute in his beliefs about ownership of the farm. The hostel bed is only available for two more days. The social worker has to decide what to do with Herbert; in the first instance, the worker decides to examine the situation from the social psychological approach.

The SPA Process: Problem Statement

Intrapsychic Level

(a) *Manifest*: Herbert believes that he is the owner of the farm, that he is married to the owner's wife, and that she and her real husband are conspiring to deprive him of his rightful property. These beliefs seem to be false.

The farmer's wife denies Herbert's accusations resolutely and is adamant that she wants him off the land because he is trespassing, and is a nuisance and an embarrassment to her and her husband. The hostel warden considers Herbert to be a satisfactory resident, but there is no possibility of a bed being made available on a longer-term basis.

The policeman considers that he has carried out his duty of arranging for Herbert to be moved from the property, but will continue to keep an eye on him to ensure that he does not get into any further 'trouble'.

(b) *Latent*: Herbert may hold other false beliefs, as yet undiscovered. He may decide that he should take further action.

Interpersonal Level

(a) *Manifest*: Herbert has annoyed and probably frightened the farmer's wife. They have not met before, and Herbert has apparently never met her husband. Herbert seems to have no relatives or friends he might contact. He relates well to the warden but not to the wife or the policeman.

(b) *Latent*: Herbert's isolation means that either he must be left to wander about, or accommodation must be found for him. Little information as to whether his isolation is his own choice or has been imposed upon him.

Intragroup Level

(a) *Manifest*: Herbert has no apparent memberships, though the policeman referred to him as 'crazy' and a 'tramp'. The policeman, the warden and the social worker are involved by virtue of their membership in professional groups. The farmer's wife is a well-respected member of the rural community.

(b) *Latent*: Herbert will have no supporters initially for any action he might choose to take in the situation. Power is vested in those groups who have intervened; the consensus is that Herbert should be 'dealt with', that is, placed in a setting where his behaviour is tolerated.

Intergroup Level

(a) *Manifest*: There is general agreement among the representatives of the various groups concerned that Herbert cannot be permitted to continue pestering the farmer. Suggestion has been made that a member of the psychiatric group should become involved.

(b) *Latent*: Involving a psychiatrist may solve the problem by removing Herbert to a hospital and would involve little effort on the social worker's part. The psychiatric group is usually dominant in dealing with mental disorders. Should Herbert not receive a psychiatric disposal and become violent or self-punitive, the social worker may well be held responsible.

Problem Analysis: Targets

The environment: The environment has a fairly central role in the situation. The farmer's territory is being invaded without justification. Herbert seems to enjoy the opportunity of having a degree of privacy in the hostel. It seems likely that Herbert has been wandering about for some weeks, always staying in accommodation intended for animals.

Group: A powerful alliance has developed to ensure Herbert's conformity to social norms. The social worker is currently the nominated leader but only by virtue of the role, particularly in having access to resources. Decision-making has been delegated to the worker with considerable freedom to manoeuvre, but within the expectation that the worker will ensure that this or a similar situation will not recur. Should the worker fail, considerable pressure will be exacted by other members of the group to remove the practitioner as the delegated worker probably through informal channels in the worker's employing agency.

Relationship: Herbert is seen as a crazy but harmless tramp, stereotype, perhaps blocking closer examination of Herbert as an individual. Would the worker be as sure in the assessment of him on the information available if Herbert were the local magistrate?

In attributing a reason for Herbert's actions, the worker has concentrated almost solely on Herbert's character: no one else to the worker's knowledge has made the same allegations and Herbert repeats his assertions despite evidence to the contrary. However, the worker has not checked whether he has made this allegation about anyone else (if he has not, why this couple?). The worker's causal schemata have perhaps completed too short a circuit.

Identity: Herbert has a visible stigmatised identity. He seems to vary between playing the role and successfully passing. He can obviously pass at will, but under what conditions and for what reasons? In his contact with the worker, he has always seemed capable of adequate impression management, which may indicate that he does seek social approval. What little he says about his background indicates that fairly recently he was employed in some form of responsible capacity. He seems to be somewhere along the process linking role conflict and marginality with alienation.

Change: Potential exists for change on a substantial level, particularly financial, social and psychological. The worker can provide accommodation, social security benefits and a form of social contact (supervised bedsitter) but Herbert would have to exhibit an amount of psychological change before he would benefit, though this may well occur as a result of these other forms of change taking place first. Herbert intends to stay in the area but pressure is apparent that he should either move elsewhere or stay locally under supervision. Some work might be necessary to persuade the farmer and policeman to tolerate Herbert's presence in the interim.

Problem Explanation: Key Processes

Construal: Aspects of Herbert's construal system conflict with social 'reality' are not amenable to disconfirmation. The generation of this "unacceptable construal system is unknown". A decision needs to be made whether this should be controlled, treated, ignored or redirected. At the moment Herbert does not wish to be 'treated' and has done nothing to merit formal control. His unacceptable construals need to be either ignored or redirected. The construal systems of the others involved are identical in evaluating him as 'mad'.

Consistency: Herbert is consistent in his assertions; his thoughts, feelings and actions are balanced and not amenable to internal threat. It seems likely that he has held the beliefs for some time.

Comparison: His beliefs receive no confirmation. In fact, the more he asserts his beliefs, the greater the attempts at invalidation by others. How much does his belief stem from an attempt at differentiation? Why does he need to? Is he receiving confirmation of his belief from any source?

Conformity: Herbert readily conforms to environments imposed upon him. He also insists that others conform to his unacceptable views. If people are continually exposed to his views and fail to conform, will his construal be ultimately invalidated, particularly if alternative and more acceptable construals are offered in their stead?

For Herbert, massive potential conflict exists between his construals, his search for comparison and his drive for conformity. Potential for change is also therefore considerable.

Change and Techniques for Change

	Change	*Technique*
1.	Place Herbert in a supervised bedsitter with adequate social contacts	Negotiate with housing association and voluntary agency
2.	Reinforce the acceptable aspects of his construal system	Develop structured relationship
3.	Provide opportunity for unacceptable constructs to be continually invalidated	Persuade farmer and wife to continue contact, but in Herbert's own environment
4.	Develop series of hypotheses about the factors that maintain Herbert's behaviour and put them to the test	Theory building
5.	As interim measure, consider keeping Herbert away from the farm by developing reward/sanction system	Behaviour modification techniques
6.	As long-stop prepare way for hospital admission, should his behaviour become dangerous	Anticipate the possible need to use coercion, and select the means least damaging to Herbert beforehand
7.	Seek information about previous group memberships and attempt his reintroduction to those or similar groups	Attitude change techniques focus: (i) Herbert (ii) leaders of relevant groups

Reflexive Analysis

The worker has found it difficult to examine Herbert's behaviour without looking through a stereotype of the sort of people who become 'tramps', and has an inclination to adopt one of the medical models as an explanatory frame. However, at the moment, the worker has no reason or need to interpret Herbert's behaviour as 'schizophrenic', 'personality disorder' or whatever---such attributed concepts may distort rather than add to the analysis, given the actual behaviour observed and the information available. The worker's experience indicates a pessimistic view of the likely outcome of the interventions, based largely on previous failures to change the attitudes of enough colleagues to assist in such planned change. The sense of pessimism may also stem, in some measure, from the worker's fear of being seen as a non-conformer or an idealist by colleagues. Should the worker attempt to work jointly with one particular colleague, perhaps a social work assistant, from the outset of this case?

This record from mental health field has been reproduced/quoted to acquaint the readers with this new and innovative model. For further details, please consult *Social Work: The Social Psychological Approach* by Breakwell and Rowett (1982).

Bibliography

Ackerman, Nathan W. (1958), *The Psychodynamics of Family Life*, New York: Basic Books.

Artherton, C.R. et al (1971), Locating Points for Intervention, *Social Case Work* (March), p. 228.

Austin, Lucille (1950), "Differential Trends in Social Case Work", in *Principles and Techniques in Social Case Work*, New York: FSAA.

Bartlett, Harriet M. (1970), *The Common Base of Social Work Practice*, New York: NASW, p. 100.

Becker, H.S. (1974), Labelling Theory Reconsidered in Rock and McIntosh (eds.), *Deviance and Social Control*, London.

Bernard, Viola W. (1964), "The University Medical Centre as a Setting for Training in Community Psychiatry," in Leopold Bellak (ed.), *Hand Book of Community Psychiatry and Community Mental Health*, New York: Grune & Straton, pp. 97-121.

Bickley, Walter (1967), *Sociology and Modern Systems Theory*, Englewood Cliffs, New Jersey: Prentice Hall.

Biestek, Felix (1957), *The Casework Relationship*, Chicago: Loyola University Press, pp. 4-12.

Bisno, H. (1969), quoted by Compton and Galaway (1975), *Social Work Processes*, Homewood (Illinois): The Dorsey Press, p. 8.

Boehm, Werner W. (1958), The Nature of Social Work, *Social Work*, Vol. 3: 2 (April), pp. 10-18.

--- (1959), *The Social Case Work Method in Social Work Education*, New York: Council on Social Work Education.

Bowers, Swithun (1949), The Nature and Definition of Social Case Work, *Social Case Work*, 30 (December), pp. 4-17.

Brenner quoted by Strean, H.S. (1979), *Psychoanalytic Theory and Social Work Practice*, New York: Free Press, p. 21.

Bruno, F.J. (1957), *Trends in Social Work Practice: 1874-1956*, New York: Columbia University Press.

Cameron, W.R. (1961), Country Psychiatric Emergency, *Publ. Health, Rep.* 76: 4: pp. 357-60.

Caplan, Gerald (1951), A Public Health Approach to Child Psychiatry, *Mental Health*, 35, p. 235.

Colwell, Catherine and Post, Felix (1963), "Community Needs of Elderly Psychiatric Patients," in Hugh Freeman, D. P.M. and James Farnadale, Ph.D., F.H.A. (eds)., *Trends in the Mental Health Services*, Oxford: Pergamon Press, pp. 251-60.

Compton, B.L. and Galaway, B. (1975), *Social Work Processes*, Homewood (Illinois): The Dorsey Press, p. 11.

Coopersmith, S. (1967), *The Antecedents of Self Esteem*, New York: W.H. Freeman Co.

Coyle, Grace L. (1948), *Group Work with American Youth*, New York: Harper and Row, p. 91.

Daniel, E.O., Keefe (1960), "Psychiatric Social Work," *Social Work Year Book*, pp. 451-460.

David, Ann P. (1965), Social Work in an American Mental Hospital: A Brief Survey, *Indian Journal of Psychiatry*, 7, pp. 151-155.

Dewald quoted by Sant Singh (1968), *Transference* (A cyclostyled paper), Varanasi Vidyapith.

Dobzhansky, T. (1976), The Genetic Predestination and Tabula Race Myths, *Perspectives in Biology and Medicine*, 19: 2.

Ellis, A. (1973b), *Humanistic Psychotherapy: The Rational Emotive Approach*, New York: Julian Press.

Erikson, Erik H. (1950), *Childhood and Society*, New York: WW Norton, Chapter VII.

Fabun Dan (1960), *Communications: The Transfer of Meaning*, Beverly Hills, Glancoe Press, p. 5.

Family Service Association of America (1953), *Scope and Methods of the Family Service Agency*, New York: FSAA.

Ferriera, A.C. and Winter, W.D. (1965), Family Interaction and Decision Making, *Arch. Gen. phychiat*: 13, pp. 214-23.

French, Lois Meredith (1940), *Psychiatric Social Work*, New York: Commonwealth Fund, p. 12.

Freud, Sigmund (1964), *An Outline of Psychoanalysis*, Standard Kl., Vol. 23, London: Hogerth, p. 201.

Fromm, Erich (1956), *The Art of Loving*, New York: Harper and Brothers, p. 47.

Germain, C. and Gitterman, A. (1970), "The Life Model of Social Work Practice," in Turner (ed.), *Social Work Treatment*, New York: Free Press, pp. 361-84.

Goffman, E. (1968), *Asylums,* Harmondsworth: Penguin.

Goldstein, Howard (1973), *Social Work Practice: A Unitary Approach*, Columbia: University of South Carolina Press, p. 31.

Grinker, Roy R. et al (1961), *Psychiatric Social Work: A Transactional Case Book*, New York: Basic Books Inc.

Grosser, Charles F. (1976), *New Direction in Community Organisation*, New York: Praeger Press, p. 10.

Hallowitz, David (1967), The Assertive Counselling Component of Therapy, *Social Case Work*, 48 (November), pp. 545-48.

---- (1979), "Problem Solving Theory" in Turner (ed.), *Social Work Treatment*, New York: Free Press.

Hamilton, Gordon (1951), *Theory and Practice of Social Case Work*, New York: Columbia University Press.

---- (1958), "A Theory of Personality: Freud's Contribution to Social Work" in Howard J. Parad (ed.), *Ego Psychology and Dynamic Case Work*, New York: Family Service Association of America.

Haralambos, M. and Heald, R. (1980), *Sociology*, Delhi: Oxford University Press, p. 281.

Hearn, Gordon (1968), *The General Systems Approach*, New York: CSWE.

Heckhausen, H. (1967), *The Anatomy of Achievement Motivation*, New York: Academic Press.

Hollis, Florence (1972), *Casework: A Psychosocial Therapy*, New York: Random House.

Jammu, P.S. (1986), Development in Rural Areas: An Overview, Regional Seminar, Hissar: HAU-Feb.

Johnson, Louise C. (1983), *Social Work Practice: A Generalist Approach*, Boston, Allyn and Bacon.

Johnson, Wendell (1951), Being Understanding and Understood, *ETC*, 8: 3, Spring, pp. 171-79.

Kahn, R. and Connell, C. (1957), *The Dynamics of Interviewing*, New York: Wiley, p. 57.

Kaith-Lucas, A. (1972), *The Giving and Taking of Help*, Chapel Hill, N.C., University of North Carolina Press, p. 103.

Korner, I.N. (1973), "Crisis Reduction and the Psychological Consultant", in Specter and Claiborn (eds.), *Crisis Intervention*, New York: Behavioural Publications, p. 30.

Linton, Ralph (1945), "Present World Conditions in Cultural Perspective," in Linton (ed.), *The Science of Men in World Crisis*, New York: Columbia University Press.

Lowry, Ferm (1936), The Clients Needs: Social Casework Treatment in *The Differential Approach in Casework Treatment*', New York: FWAA, pp. 1-13.

Maier, N.R.J. (1965), *Psychology in Industry*, Boston: Houghton Mifflin.

Marfatia, J.C. et al (1963), The Child Guidance Clinic and Research Centre, *Prabha-Journal of the Gujarat Research Society*: 25, pp. 14-20.

Maslow, A.H. (1954), *Motivation and Personality*, New York: Harper and Row.

May, A.R., Sheldon, A.P. and Mackeith, S.A. (1962), Future of District Psychiatry, *Lancet*: 2, pp. 1319-20.

Mowrer, O.H. (1950), *Learning Theory and Personality Dynamics*, New York: Ronald Press.

Nayyer, Sushila (1965), Inaugural Address, Second Meeting of Mental Health Advisory Committee, Ranchi, November 8, 1965.

Northen, Helen (1959), *Social Work with Groups*, New York: Columbia University Press, pp. 53-58.

Parad, Howard J., Lola Selby, Jones Quinlan (1976), "Crisis Intervention with Families and Groups" in Roberts and Northen (eds.), *Theories of Social Work with Groups*, New York: Columbia University Press, pp. 304-30.

Parsons, Talcott (1951), *The Social System*, Glencoe, Illinois: Free Press.

Perlman, Helen (1957), *Social Case Work: A Problem Solving Process*, Chicago: University of Chicago Press.

--- (1962), "Intake and Some Role Considerations" in Cora Kassius (ed.), *Social Casework in the Fifties*, New York: FSAA, pp. 163-74.

— (1979), *Relationship: The Art of Helping People*, Chicago: University of Chicago Press, p. 57.

Perls, F. et al (1958), *Gestalt Therapy*, New York: Julian Press.

Pincus and Minahan (1970), quoted by Goldstein, H. (1973), *Social Work Practice*, Columbia: University of South Carolina Press, p. 50.

--- (1973), *Social Work Practice: Model and Method*, Itasca (Illinois): FE Peacock, p. 9 and 15.

Pray, Kenneth, L.M. (1949), *Social Work in a Revolutionary Age*, Philadelphia: University of Pennsylvania Press.

Ramanshyn, John M. (1971), *Social Welfare: From Charity to Social Justice*, New York: Random House (CSWE), p. 4.

Rapoport, L. (1969), "Social Case Work: An Appraisal and an Affirmation", *Smith College Studies in Social Work*, 39: 225 (June).

Regensburg, Jeannette (1938), An Attempt to See Casework Apart from the Related Professions, *AAPSW Newsletter*, 7: 4.

Reid, William J. (1978), *The Task-Centred System*, New York: Columbia University Press.

Richmond, Mary (1917), *Social Diagnosis*, New York: Russell Sage Foundation, pp. 211-15.

---- (1922), *What is Social Case Work?* New York: Russell Sage Foundation, pp. 98-99.

Robinson, V.P. (1942), Training for Skill in Social Case Work, *Journal of Social Work Process*: 4.

Rogers, Carl R. (1954), *Psychotherapy and Personality Change*, Chicago: University of Chicago Press.

---- (1966), "Client-Centered Therapy", in Patterson (ed.), *Theories of Counselling and Psychotherapy*, New York: Harper and Row.

Rosen, B.C. and D'Andrade, R. (1959), The Psychosocial Origins of Achievement Motivation, *Sociometry*, 1959, 22 (3) September.

Ross, Murray G., (1967), *Community Organisation*, New York: Harper and Row, p. 39.

Scherz, Frances, H. (1970), Theories and Practice of Family Therapy in Roberts and Nee (eds.), *Theories of Social Case Work*: Chicago: The University of Chicago Press.

Schertz (1951 & 1970), quoted by Compton and Galaway, *Social Work Processes*, Homewood (Illinois): The Dorsey Press, p. 8.

Selly, Lola G. (1963), Social Work and Crisis, *Social Work Papers*, Vol. 10, Los Angeles: University of Southern California.

Siporin, Max (1975), *Introduction to Social Work Practice*, New York: Mc Millian.

Sheeley, William F. (1952), "Family Physician, State Hospital and Community," an address to the New Mexico Medical Society, Las Vegas, New Mexico, March 11.

Skidmore, R.A. and Thackery, M.G. (1982), *An Introduction to Social Work*, New Jersey: Prentice Hall, p. 59.

Skinner, B.F. (1938), *The Behaviour of Organisms*, New York, Appleton Century Crofts.

Skinner, B.F. (1953), *Science and Human Behaviour*, New York, Macmillan Co.

Smalley, Ruth E. (1967): *Theory for Social Work Practice*, New York, Columbia University Press.

Spiegel, John (1971), *Transactions: The Interplay Between Individuals, Family & Society*, New York: Science House.

Swanson, Mary G. and Woolson, Allen M. (1973), Psychotherapy with the Unmotivated Patient in *Psychotherapy: Theory, Research and Practice*, p. 77.

Taber, L.R. and Taber, R.H. (1985), "Social Casework" in Fink et al (eds.), *The Fields of Social Work*, London: Sage Foundation, p. 178.

Taft, Jessie (1937), The Relation of Function to Process in Social Casework, *Journal of Social Work Process*, 1: 1, p. 8.

Timms, Noel (1964), *Social Casework*, London: Routledge and Kegan Paul.

Thomas, E.J. et al (1960), *In-Service Training and Reduced Work Loads*, New York: Russell Sage Foundation, pp. 107-10.

Thomas, Edwin J. (1968), *The Socio-Behavioural Approach and Applications to Social Work*, New York: CSWE.

Towle, Charlotte (1945), *Common Human Needs*, Washington D.C.: Government Printing Office.

Turner, Francis, J. (ed.) (1968), *Differential Diagnosis and Treatment in Social Work*, New York: Free Press.

Upadhyay, R.K. (1993), *Indian Philosophical Concepts in Clinical Social Work*, Kurukshetra University, p. 78.

Walsh, D. (1972), quoted by Haralambos and Heald (1980), *Sociology*, Delhi: Oxford University Press.

Weber, Max (1864-1920), quoted in *Social Science Encyclopedia*, London, Routledge & Kegan Paul.

Wolberg, Lewis R. (1954), *The Techniques of Psychotherapy*, New York: Grune and Straton.

WHO Report of Committee, B. (1959), Community Psychiatric Services (cyclostyled document, unpublished), Conference on Mental Hygiene Practice, Helsinki.

Yapp, Bridget G. (1959), "Work of the Psychiatric Social Worker", in W. Marry Burbery, Edna M. Baling, Bridget J. Yapp (written), *An Introduction to Child Guidance*, London, Mcmillan and Co., pp. 99-110.

Zastrow, Charles (1978), *Introduction to Social Welfare Institutions*, H.C. Wood (Illinois): The Dorsey Press, p. 443.

Index